WHO, WHERE, AND WHAT IS GOD?

God as architect of the universe. Codex Vindobonensis 2554 (French, ca. 1250). In the Österreichische Nationalbibliothek, Vienna.

WHO, WHERE, AND WHAT IS GOD?

ALBERTUS PRETORIUS

WIPF & STOCK · Eugene, Oregon

WHO, WHERE, AND WHAT IS GOD?

Copyright © 2022 Albertus Pretorius. All rights reserved. Except for brief quotations in critical publications or reviews, no part of this book may be reproduced in any manner without prior written permission from the publisher. Write: Permissions, Wipf and Stock Publishers, 199 W. 8th Ave., Suite 3, Eugene, OR 97401.

Wipf & Stock
An Imprint of Wipf and Stock Publishers
199 W. 8th Ave., Suite 3
Eugene, OR 97401

www.wipfandstock.com

PAPERBACK ISBN: 978-1-6667-3825-4
HARDCOVER ISBN: 978-1-6667-9870-8
EBOOK ISBN: 978-1-6667-9871-5

CONTENTS

Chapter		Page
	Foreword	vii
	Introduction	1
Part A:	**The Biblical Cosmology**	**5**
1.	Prescientific Biblical Concepts	7
2.	The Hebrew Concept of the Cosmos	9
3.	The Early Christian View of the Cosmos	31
4.	The Qur'an	58
5.	The Clash of Science and Theology	61
Part B:	**Deconstruction**	**71**
6.	The Contemporary View of God	73
7.	Efforts to Prove the Existence of God	80
8.	Attempts to Show the Improbability of God's Existence	84
9.	A God Unworthy of Worship	95
10.	The Impossibility that God ever Existed	104
Part C:	**Reconstruction**	**131**
11.	The Scientific Method	133
12.	Axioms	149
13.	Fundamentals of Ethics	164
14.	The Mind of God	182
15.	The Human Spirit, Soul and Body	194
16.	Afterword	202
Bibliography		**207**

List of Illustrations

God as Architect of the Universe	ii
The Beit Alpha Mosaic	12
The Hebrew Conception of the Cosmos	21
The Aristotelian Worldview	38
Frontispiece to Galileo's *Dialogo*	62
How our Solar System Fits into the Bigger Picture of the Universe	68
Plato	114
The Human Brain	174

FOREWORD

This book is the result of a lifetime of study – theology, philosophy, history and psychology.

It is with a certain measure of trepidation and hesitation that this book is being presented to the world. I am very conscious of the fact that I am contradicting the beliefs of many people who hold firm religious views and whose faith is something dear to them. I have seen countless cases where a religious faith helped people to find meaning in life and to find guidance in the struggle between good and bad and right and wrong. Many people have found emotional and social support in their religious communities.

This book cannot but undermine those beliefs and I feel sorry for those people who might go through an intellectual and emotional struggle when they consider the evidence presented in this book.

However, it cannot be helped. I feel compelled to disclose the results of my investigations, ruminations, and own struggles and in the process unmask certain superstitions and even religious hypocrisy and fraud. If I don't do it, I won't be true to myself.

Albertus Pretorius, February 2022

INTRODUCTION

Christians gather in a church on a Sunday, Jews have their meetings in a synagogue on a Saturday and Muslims pray on a Friday in a mosque. The adherents of each of these monotheistic religions partake in these gatherings with one overriding goal: they wish to worship a supreme being, called God.

During these gatherings they pray, read from the sacred scriptures, listen to sermons and sing Psalms and hymns. All these activities are centered around the worship of a God who is regarded as the creator of the universe, the law-giver and the sustainer of all that exists.

Whenever a believer of one of these religions is asked what he or she means when he or she mentions the word "God" (or "Allah" in Arabic) he or she will immediately respond that one has to look in the sacred scriptures to find out who, where and what God is. These scriptures are the Bible – of which Jews only read the first part, called the "Old Testament" by Christians – or the Qur'an.

We may, though, ask: Do these scriptures really give us a satisfactory answer to this question: who, where, and what is God?

This book will demonstrate that the way the holy scriptures describe the creator and supreme being differs fundamentally from the way believers of the 21st century think about him. The scriptures contain naïve, prescientific and primitive notions about God, the cosmos and man's place in it all, which believers of our age cannot accept anymore.

It will be demonstrated with new and original arguments that the more modern concept of God held by believers of our time is also irrational, impossible, and untenable. This God is totally absent, gone. He just never existed.

It will be shown that God is not a "who", a person who can communicate with human beings, who gets angry when people displease him, who becomes jealous when people worship other gods, who cares for his children, who hears their prayers, and who is willing to forgive people their transgressions. He cannot exist and never existed – except in the minds of believers.

There are, though, eternal, rational, and divine principles, laws and axioms that govern the universe and the social life of intelligent beings, which may be equated with the mind of an impersonal entity, which may replace the God worshipped by believers of our age. It is, therefore, possible to provide an answer to the question: where and what is God?

It is, therefore, high time that we revise, deconstruct, and reconstruct our mental pictures of God. There is no superhuman intelligent being sitting on the clouds who looks down on human beings on the earth's surface. The universe, though, is constructed rationally and logically and we may identify the underlying beautiful, eternal, and immutable principles that govern everything and acknowledge their beauty, power, and authority in amazement and wonder and perhaps recognize them as divine since they rule the universe.

It is first of all necessary that the Bible be scrutinised to find out how the people in anient biblical times regarded God, as well as other concepts that play a role in religious thought, such as heaven and earth, angels, stars and planets, spirits and souls. The Qur'an must also be investigated in this regard.

Thereafter, the current notions regarding God and the cosmos have to be illuminated and it will be shown that this conventional concept of God cannot be accepted anymore, due to the many inner contradictions and improbabilities and impossibilities it contains.

In conclusion, the "mind" of an impersonal God containing all the eternal principles and axioms that rule the universe will be described and the outlines of a new rational philosophy will be explained.

PART A
THE BIBLICAL COSMOLOGY

CHAPTER 1
PRESCIENTIFIC BIBLICAL CONCEPTS

God, Heaven, Angels, Hell, World, Stars, Spirits, and Souls
Before we can provide the proof that God is really absent and never existed, it is necessary to get clarity about another question: what do people usually understand when they use or hear the word 'God'? Most believers will immediately answer that one has only to read what the holy scriptures tell us in this regard. It is, therefore, necessary to take a good look at how the authors of the scriptures conceptualised key religious concepts such as *God, heaven, angel, hell, world, star, spirit,* and *soul*. It amounts to an investigation into the cosmology prevalent in biblical times. It is also necessary to investigate how the Qur'an describes these concepts.

Believers also easily assume that when they find these words in the Bible – or the Qur'an – that the authors of these scriptures attached the same meanings to these words and had similar mental pictures of these concepts as believers of our age. An analysis of the ways in which these words are used in the Bible shows, however, that this is not the case. People in biblical times had very different ideas regarding these words and concepts. Their conceptions were unsophisticated, concrete, and prescientific and no educated Christian or believer of our age can identify with that way of conceptualising anymore. The same goes for the Qur'an.

When Christians of our time talk about God they usually mean a spiritual (*i e* non-material) being who is not part of the observable universe since he is seen as the creator of the universe. When they utilize the word *world* they think of our planet travelling around the sun and revolving on its own axis. When modern Christians think of *angels* they visualize spiritual beings who dwell with God in *heaven*, a realm outside our universe and occupying other dimensions than the dimensions of space and time that we occupy, although they appeared on occasion in human or visible form in biblical times.

When Christians hear the word *hell,* they get a picture of a place or condition where the souls of godless and evil people are being punished. Informed Christians think of *stars* as celestial bodies similar to our sun, only much further away and therefore appearing as faint dots of light in the sky. When Christians mention *spirits*, they think of non-material entities, usually the aspect of a person that survives death, either in heaven or hell, but there may also be pure spiritual beings, such as angels and demons. When the concept of *soul* is used it is assumed that it is the inner core of a person, all the invisible faculties and characteristics of that person. The soul is also supposed to survive death and the words *spirit* and *soul* are often used as synonyms.

All these words are often encountered in the Bible. A careful analysis will show that people in biblical times attached very different meanings to all these concepts in comparison with today's usage and that our current images of these concepts actually differ fundamentally from those held in biblical times – and also in the Qur'an.

CHAPTER 2

THE HEBREW CONCEPT OF THE COSMOS

The Babylonian Cosmos
Most of the Hebrew Scriptures, called the "Old Testament" by Christians, were created or finalised only after the Babylonian exile and the Hebrew Bible only got its ultimate form in the second century BC with the inclusion of the book of Daniel.[1] During this exile, which formally ended in 538 BC, the elite of the Judeans were exposed to the most advanced civilisation of the day and that exerted a profound influence on their religious views as expressed in their scriptures.[2]

The Babylonians and their Mesopotamian predecessors, the Sumerians and the Chaldeans, were the first people to observe the skies systematically and to leave records of their observations of the stars and the weather patterns. They found that there were seven moving bodies across the skies, which they called planets, namely the sun, the moon, Mercury, Venus, Mars, Jupiter and Saturn (to use their current Latin/English names). They dedicated a separate day to each of these planets and thereby created the seven-day week – which was taken over by the Jews and which is still in use today. We still name the days of the week after these planets and we can recognise names such as Sunday, Mo(o)nday and Satur(n)day.

These celestial bodies were deemed to be gods and were worshipped as such. The astronomers/astrologers of Mesopotamia were also priests since observing the skies – and the gods – was

---

[1] Armstrong, *The Bible,* 31–43.
[2] Encyclopaedia Britannica, "Babylonian Exile".

primarily a religious activity.[3] The current Latin/English names of the five outer planets are translations of Greek, Egyptian, and Mesopotamian names and are also the names of ancient deities.

The planets were seen to move against the background of the so-called fixed stars. These fixed stars were grouped into constellations and they represented personages, animals and inanimate objects. We still use the Greek and Latin names for these constellations. Some were supposed to depict divine beings like Perseus, Andromeda, Orion, the Twins (Gemini – Castor and Pollux) and Hercules. Others were seen as celestial personages, such as Virgo (the Virgin), Ophiuchus (the Snake Catcher), Aquarius (the Water Carrier) and Boötes (the Ploughman).

Other mythological figures were: Pegasus (the Winged Horse), Cetus (the Sea Monster), Centaurus (the Centaur or a being with the upper body of a man and the lower body of a horse) and Sagittarius (the Archer – also in the form of a centaur). Other animals are Leo (the Lion), Aquila (the Eagle), Capricornus (the Goat with a fish tail), Ursa Major (the Big Bear), Scorpius (the Scorpion), Serpens (the Serpent) and Pisces (the Fishes). Inanimate objects included Scutum (the Shield), Ara (the Altar), Eridanus (the Celestial River) and Crater (the Chalice). These stars and constellations were deemed to be unchanging and eternal.

The Mesopotamians found that the sun moved through twelve of these constellations in a year's time and, therefore, these constellations received special attention. They form the so-called Zodiac – meaning circle of living beings – and they divided the year into twelve months. Each month more or less coincided with the period between two successive new moons. The Jews adopted the

---

[3] Thiel, *And then there was Light*, 35; Malina, *On the Genre and Message of Revelation*, 2–10.

Mesopotamian year of twelve months (moons) and today we still divide the year into twelve portions.[4]

The Mesopotamians were not the only people who regarded the stars and the constellantions as deities. The Egyptians based their calendar on the appearance of Sirius in Canis Major (the Big Dog) as the sign that their new year started. The stars and planets were also regarded as gods who influenced events on earth. Sirius was depicted as a goddess, Sopher, a woman with a star on her head.[5]

Adoption of Babylonian system by the Jews
The Jews adopted the Babylonian celestial constellations and regarded them as real entities. In Job 9: 9 and 38: 31–32 we read of the Zodiac (Hebrew: מַזָּרוֹת – *Mazzarot* – a word derived from "sunrise"), the Bear (Ursa Major), Orion (the Hunter) and the Pleiades (the Seven Sisters), a star cluster inside Taurus (the Bull). Orion and the Pleiades are also mentioned in Amos 5: 8. The "fleeing serpent" in "the heavens" is mentioned in Job 26: 13, and with that the constellation of Serpens (the Serpent) is meant. Serpens was traditionally associated with the snake of Genesis 3, the serpent that lured Adam and Eve into eating the forbidden fruit.[6]

Jeremiah 44: 17–19 mentions the "queen of the sky". It is not quite sure what this means – it may well refer to the moon or to the planet Venus, that is, Astarte of the Israelites' pagan neighbours. In Second Kings 17: 30 a pagan deity "Nergal" is mentioned; this was the Mesopotamian name for the constellation of Sagittarius.[7]

---

[4] Gauquelin, *Astrology and Science,* 101–03; Peters, *The Harvest of Hellenism,* 437–39; Thiel, *And then there was Light,* 43–44; Hengel, *Judentum und Hellenismus,* 432–33; McGregor and Purdy, *Jew and Greek,* 291–92,
[5] Oakes and Gahlin, *Ancient Egypt,* 116, 331.
[6] Allen, *Star Names,* 375.
[7] Allen, *Star Names,* 354.

The people who hid the so-called Dead Sea Scrolls in a series of caves near Qumran in Palestine during the Jewish war of AD 66–70 against the Romans definitely adopted and adapted the Babylonian astrology. They had, among others, an astrological calendar naming the twelve constellations in the Zodiac by their Hebrew or Aramaic names. This document was dated to the last decades of the first century BC. They removed the pagan elements from the names and the descriptions of these constellations in order to avoid any form of pagan idolatry.[8]

The Beit Alpha mosaic with Hebrew names for the different constellations of the Zodiac. The seasons are depicted on the corners.

---

[8] Jacobus, "The Zodiac Sign Names".

The Jews still adhered to the Babylonian Zodiac a few centuries into the Christian era. Archaeologists have found mosaic floors of ancient synagogues in the country of Israel depicting the Zodiac, with Hebrew names for the different constellations. The mosaic in the Beit Alpha synagogue (sixth century AD) is the best known.[9]

There are indications that the Jews attached certain signs of the Zodiac to each of the twelve tribes of Israel. That each tribe had its own sign or banner already in New Testament times may be deduced from Rev 5: 5 where we read of "the Lion who is of the tribe of Judah."

The Jewish rabbis seemed to have used more than one system of connecting the tribes with the Zodiacal signs in the past, but the following seems to be the most satisfactory system, while keeping in mind the blessings Jacob gave his twelve sons before his death, as recorded in Genesis 49:

- Gad (Aries – the Ram) (טלה - *ṭaleh*)
  "Gad, a troop will press on him; but he will press on their heel" (Gen 49: 19).

- Ephraim (Taurus – the Bull) (שור - *shor*)
  "The arms of his hands were made strong, By the hands of the Mighty One of Jacob, from there is the shepherd, the stone of Israel" (Gen 49: 24).
  "His horns are the horns of the wild-ox: With them he shall push the peoples all of them, [even] the ends of the earth: they are the ten thousands of Ephraim" (Deut 3: 17).

- Simeon (Gemini – the Twins) (תאומים - *te'umim*)

---

[9] Dennis, "Jewish Myth".

"Simeon and Levi are brothers; weapons of violence are their swords" (Gen 49: 6).

- Levi (Gemini – the Twins) (תאומים - *te'umim*)
  "Simeon and Levi are brothers; weapons of violence are their swords" (Gen 49: 6).

- Issachar (Cancer – the Crab) (סרטן - *sarṭan*)
  "He saw a resting-place, that it was good, the land, that it was pleasant; He bowed his shoulder to bear, and became a servant doing forced labor" (Gen 49: 14).

- Judah (Leo – the Lion) (אריה - *arieh*)
  "Judah is a lion's whelp" (Gen 49: 9) (see also Rev 5: 5).

- Asher (Virgo – the Virgin) (בתולה - *betulah*)
  "Out of Asher his bread will be fat, he will yield royal dainties" (Gen 49: 20).

- Benjamin (Libra – the Weighing Scales) (מאזנים - *moznayim*)
  "Benjamin is a ravenous wolf. In the morning she will devour the prey. At evening he will divide the spoil" (Gen 49: 27).

- Dan (Scorpius – the Scorpion) (עקרב - *'aḳrab*)
  "Dan will be a serpent in the way, an adder in the path" (Gen 49: 17).

- Manasseh (Sagittarius – the Archer) (קשת - *ḳeshet*)
  "The archers have sorely grieved him, shot at him, and persecute him. But his bow abode in strength" (Gen 49: 22–24).

- Naphtali (Capricorn – the Goat) (גדי - *ğedi*)
  "Naphtali is a doe set free, who bears beautiful fawns." (Gen 49: 21).

- Reuben (Aquarius – the Water Carrier) (דלי - *deli*)
  "Boiling over as water, you shall not have the pre-eminence" (Gen 49: 4).

- Zebulun (Pisces – the Fishes) (דגים - *dagim*)
  "Zebulun will dwell at the haven of the sea" (Gen 49: 13).[10]

The Babylonians had extensive creation myths and the biblical authors adopted those myths, albeit with some significant alterations. The best-known creation myth in the Bible is to be found in Genesis 1. Where the Babylonians regarded the sun, moon, planets and stars as gods, the Hebrew Bible stressed the view that their God, Yahweh, created all these bodies.

The Jews thought that the planets, stars and constellations were angels and cherubs, instead of gods – which actually amounts to more or less the same. In Job 38: 4–8 we are told that when the foundations of the earth were laid by God, "the morning stars sang together, and all the sons of God shouted for joy." The "sons of God" are, of course, the angels – and they are equated with the stars. Ps 148: 2–3 contains this call: "Praise him, all his angels! Praise him, all his host! Praise him, sun and moon! Praise him, all you shining stars!" That means that the angels, the host of heaven and the astrological bodies were seen to be the same entities. Nehemiah 9: 6 assures us that God created everything, including the "host" of stars and that "the host of heaven" worships God.

---

[10] Allen, *Star Names*, 48, 78, 108, 138, 223, 253, 273, 339, 352, 362, 381, 464.

Influence of the Stars
The Sumerian, Chaldean and Babylonian priests and astrologers studied the skies in order to find out what the intentions of the gods in the sky were regarding the fate of kingdoms, kings and other important people. They drew up horoscopes in which the positions of the sun and other planets against the constellations of the Zodiac and the horizon were plotted. That helped important people to make decisions regarding auspicious days on which to start new ventures and how to avert potential dangers.[11]

The Hebrew Scriptures seem to hold the same view. In Job 38: 33, this question is asked: "Do you know the laws of the heavens? Can you establish the dominion of it over the earth?" This question presupposes the view of ancient pagan astrology that events on earth are being influenced by the stars in heaven. Jeremiah 31: 35 mentions "the ordinances of the moon and of the stars", which were given by God. We also read of God's "ordinances of heaven and earth" in Jer 33: 25. These expressions suggest the rules according to which the ancient astrologers interpreted the divine intentions.

Hebrew View of Heaven and Earth
The Hebrew word for *heaven* is שָׁמַיִם (*shamayim*). This word was used in more than one way and has more than one meaning, namely the sky (containing the atmosphere and the clouds), the starry heaven and the abode of God. It has to be pointed out that this word is used only in the plural form and, therefore, it should actually be translated as 'heavens' – encompassing the firmament, the stars in heaven and the home of God. It will become clear that the authors of the Old Testament regarded these different meanings as synonyms. For them the sky filled with clouds was essentially the same space as the starry heaven and the dwelling place of God beyond the stars.

---

[11] Malina, *On the Genre and Message of Revelation*, 2–20.

Together with the Mesopotamians, the Judeans thought of the sky or the heaven as a vault above the earth. God created the "expanse" or vault of heaven to divide the waters above and below the earth (Gen 1: 6). The author of the book of Job informs us in 22: 14 that God "walks on the vault of the sky"; that means that He was to be found immediately beyond the dome surrounding the earth and onto which the planets and the other stars are affixed. Isaiah 40: 22 tells us that God "sits above the circle of the earth, and the inhabitants of it are as grasshoppers..." The Hebrew word for "circle" (חוּג – *chug*) may also be translated as "vault" or "dome".

In various texts the idea is to be found that God spread the sky or the heavens like a sheet or a curtain over the earth (Job 9: 8; Ps 104: 2; Isa 40: 22; Isa 42: 5; Isa 44: 24; Isa 45: 12–13; Zech 12: 1). We also find the notion that God dwells between the stars: "Isn't God in the heights of heaven? See the height of the stars, how high they are!" (Job 22: 12). Ps 19: 4 calls the firmament "a tent for the sun" behind which he hides at night and comes forth in the morning "as a bridegroom coming out of his chamber". This firmament rests on pillars that are planted on earth (Job 26: 11).

The following question is posed in Isa 40: 12 – "Who has measured the waters in the hollow of his hand, and meted out the sky [alternative: heavens] with the span, and comprehended the dust of the earth in a measure, and weighed the mountains in scales, and the hills in a balance?"

The answer to this question is, of course: God. The result of all this is that the heavens as abode of God are part of the same space occupied by the earth and other celestial bodies. After all, Isa 66: 1 proclaims: "Thus says Yahweh, heaven is my throne, and the earth is my footstool." There is, therefore, continuity between heaven and earth and the cosmos is a closed system, containing God's heaven and earth.

The ancient peoples usually thought of their gods as living on a high mountain, somewhere in the north. The Sumerians thought that the throne of Anu, the god of the heavens, was situated on a high mountain or at the northern celestial pole. The Greeks saw Mount Olympus, in northern Greece and the highest mountain in Greece, as the home of their gods and the throne of Zeus, the father of the gods.[12]

Similar ideas are to be found in the Hebrew Scriptures. The king of Babylon is addressed in Isa 14: 13 –

> "You said in your heart, I will ascend into heaven, I will exalt my throne above the stars of God; and I will sit on the mountain of congregation, in the uttermost parts of the north ..."

In Job 37: 22 it is written: "Out of the north comes golden splendour; with God is awesome majesty." Isaiah 11: 9, Isa 65: 25 and Ezek 28: 14 mention God's "holy mountain" (see also Ps 48: 2–3) and Isa 2: 2 affirms that God's house is on a high mountain. We are informed by 1 Kgs 22: 19 – "I saw Yahweh sitting on his throne, and all the host of heaven standing by him on his right hand and on his left." In other words: the throne of God was thought of as situated between the stars to the north.

This identification of the throne of God with the northern celestial pole makes sense from the viewpoint of the ancient cosmology, since everything in the sky, as well as the earth, seemed to revolve around that central point.

Genesis 1: 1 reminds us that the heavens and earth were created together and at the same time, "in the beginning". Psalm 148: 4 tells us of "waters that are above the heavens". These must be regarded as the storage places of the rain and, therefore, the heaven and the sky had to have windows through which this water could be poured down upon the earth (Gen 7: 11; Gen 8: 2; 2 Kgs 7: 2; Mal 3: 10).

Various texts contain the thought that God is observing the earth and the people on the earth from the vantage point of heaven

---

[12] Cornelius, *Geistesgeschichte der Frühzeit*, 13, 35–36; Visser, *De Openbaring aan Johannes*, 57–58.

where he resides – and that is the reason why he is able to see and know everything (Gen 21: 17; Ps 14: 2; Ps 33: 13–14; Ps 102: 19).

The weather was experienced as the result of the direct intervention of God. Thunder was regarded as God's voice (2 Sam 22: 14; Job 37: 4–5; Ps 104: 7), clouds were deemed to be his clothes (Job 22: 14), rain fell when he commanded it (Ps 147: 8) and hail stones fell when he hurled them from heaven (Jos 10: 11). Ps 104: 3 declares: "He makes the clouds his chariot. He walks on the wings of the wind."

All these texts make it clear that the Judeans thought of the heaven in a very concrete way. For them the sky, the atmosphere, the starry skies and the heaven as the home of God were parts of one and the same system or space. The people who built the Tower of Babel even thought that they could erect a structure "whose top reaches to the sky" (or heavens) (Gen 11: 4). The contemporary idea that God's heaven must be somewhere outside the universe, probably in another dimension, would have been incomprehen-sible to the authors and original readers of the Old Testament books.

To summarize: there was, according to ancient Israel, no real difference between the sky with its clouds, the vault from which the stars were hanging and the dwelling place of God. For that reason they used only one word, שָׁמַיִם (*shamayim*), to name the *sky*, the *starry heavens* and the *heaven* as dwelling place of God.

The world was thought to be a flat disc that floated upon the primeval ocean (Exod 20: 4) and as such it had boundaries or an edge (Ps 74: 17). Proverbs 30: 4 mentions "all the ends of the earth" – in other words: the world had a limit or an edge where it ended. It was thought that there was water below the earth – most probably the source of the water that flowed from fountains (Deut 4: 19). Psalm 136: 6 says that God "spread out the earth above the waters." Proverbs 8: 28 mentions "the springs of the deep".

The world rests upon pillars or foundations (Ps 82: 5; Prov 8: 29; Jer 31: 37; Zech 12: 1). In 1 Sam 2: 8 we are informed: "For the pillars of the earth are Yahweh`s, He has set the world on them." Psalm

104: 5 adds: "He laid the foundations of the earth, that it should not be moved forever." Psalm 93: 1 and Ps 96: 10 both declare: "The world is also established. It can't be moved." On the other hand, the earth was deemed to be hanging in the void and Job 26: 7 says that God "stretches out the north over empty space, and hangs the earth on nothing."

Hebrew View of the Underworld

The Old Testament gave very little attention to the afterlife and it is only the late book of Daniel that contains a promise that the faithful will be resurrected at the end of time and inherit life everlasting with God in heaven. We read in Dan 12: 2–3 – "Many of those who sleep in the dust of the earth shall awake, some to everlasting life, and some to shame and everlasting contempt. Those who are wise shall shine as the brightness of the expanse; and those who turn many to righteousness as the stars forever and ever."

In other words: Daniel expected the deceased faithful to gain places in the starry skies.

For the rest, the Israelites merely expected to go to the underworld (Hebrew: שְׁאוֹל – *Sheol*) after they had died where they would experience a shadowy existence (Gen 37: 35; Gen 42: 38; Gen 29: 31; Ps 55: 16; Ezek 31: 15 *etc*). This realm of the dead was thought to be below the surface of the flat earth. Ps 63: 9 locates it in "the lower parts of the earth". Amos 9: 2 thought that it was even possible to "dig into Sheol". Whenever the Old Testament mentioned Sheol, it was made clear that the dead had to "descend" into this underworld.

In Num 16: 31–34 we read of a remarkable incident:

> "It happened, as he [Moses] made an end of speaking all these words, that the ground split apart that was under them [the rebels]; and the earth opened its mouth, and swallowed them up, and their households, and all the men who appertained to Korah [the leader of the rebel group], and all their goods. So

they, and all that appertained to them, went down alive into Sheol: and the earth closed on them, and they perished from among the assembly. All Israel that were round about them fled at the cry of them; for they said, lest the earth swallow us up."

This is, no doubt, a description of a sinkhole, a case where the earth's surface suddenly caves in and drops into a cave or hollow space below the surface. The author of this report interpreted this hole as an opening into Sheol, the abode of the dead under the earth's surface.

We read in 1 Sam 28: 7–25 how King Saul of Israel consulted an oracle of the dead, the witch of En-dor, and requested her to raise the prophet Samuel from the dead. The woman reported to Saul: "I see a god coming up out of the earth" (vs 13). The spirit of Samuel then asked Saul: "Why have you disquieted me, to bring me up?" (vs 15). The report of this episode confirms the conclusion that the Old Testament thought of Sheol as being somewhere below the earth's surface. It was, therefore, a real physical locality.

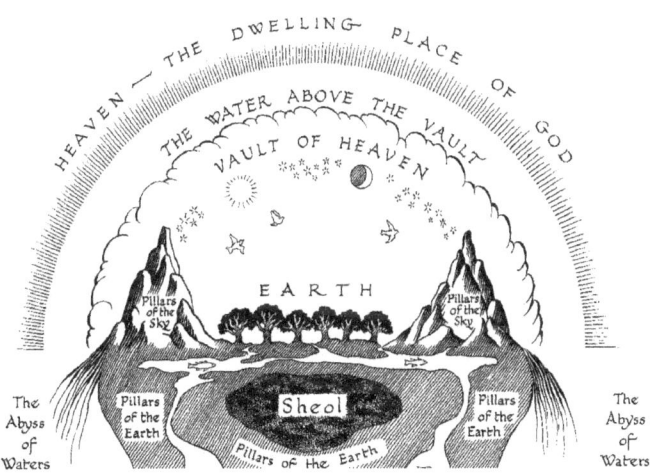

The Hebrew conception of the cosmos.

Below the surface of the earth there was also supposed to be a deep abyss, called תְּהוֹם (*tehom* – Gen 1: 2; Prov 8: 27–28). This word has many meanings: deep, depths, deep places, abyss, the deep, deep of subterranean waters, primeval ocean, the grave. This abyss encompassed the whole of the underworld.

The illustration (above) provides a simplified view of how the cosmos – the heavens, earth, the underworld and the ocean under the earth – was conceptualised by the authors of the Old Testament.

Hebrew View of God

The Hebrew Scriptures often mention that God is somehow associated with fire and light.

The evil cities of Sodom and Gomorrah were destroyed when it "rained on Sodom …. sulfur and fire from Yahweh out of the sky" (Gen 19: 24). Moses encountered God in "a flame of fire out of the midst of a bush" while tending the flocks of his father-in-law (Exod 3: 2). When the Israelites fled from slavery in Egypt, "Yahweh went before them by day in a pillar of cloud, to lead them on their way, and by night in a pillar of fire, to give them light, that they might go by day and by night" (Exod 13: 21). When Moses received the Ten Commandments from God, "Mount Sinai, the whole of it, smoked, because Yahweh descended on it in fire; and its smoke ascended like the smoke of a furnace" (Exod 19: 19). Num 16: 35 relates how "fire came forth from Yahweh, and devoured the two hundred fifty men who offered the incense."

The sun is even seen as a sign of God's presence: "For Yahweh God is a sun and a shield" (Ps 84: 11). Malachi has a similar thought: "But to you who fear my name shall the sun of righteousness arise with healing in its wings" (Mal 4: 2).

In Deut 4: 12 and 36 the Israelites were reminded: "Yahweh spoke to you out of the midst of the fire: you heard the voice of words, but you saw no form; only [you heard] a voice. (….) Out of heaven he made you to hear his voice, that he might instruct you: and on earth he made you to see his great fire; and you heard his words out of the midst of the fire". We are told in Judg 13: 20 that "the angel of Yahweh ascended in the flame of the altar".

Second Samuel 22: 9 contains the following description of God: "There went up a smoke out of his nostrils, fire out of his mouth devoured: Coals were kindled by it."

The prophet Elijah and the prophets of Baal held a contest to determine whose deity was the real God. The prophets of Baal tried their best but got no response from Baal. Elijah prayed and "the fire of Yahweh fell, and consumed the burnt offering, and the wood, and the stones, and the dust, and licked up the water that was in the trench" (1 Kgs 18: 1–38). When Elijah was taken up into heaven by God, it happened in "a chariot of fire, and horses of fire, which parted them both apart; and Elijah went up by a whirlwind into heaven" (2 Kgs 2: 11).

Daniel described Judgment Day as follows:

"I saw until thrones were placed, and one who was ancient of days sat: his clothing was white as snow, and the hair of his head like pure wool; his throne was fiery flames, [and] the wheels of it burning fire. A fiery stream issued and came forth from before him: thousands of thousands ministered to him, and ten thousand times ten thousand stood before him: the judgment was set, and the books were opened." (Dan 7: 9–10).

Job 36: 30 informs us about God: "Behold, he spreads his light around him". The following prayer is voiced in Ps 4: 7 – "Yahweh, let the light of your face shine on us." The poet of Ps 27: 1 confirms: "Yahweh is my light and my salvation". Psalm 36: 10 assures us: "In your light shall we see light." In Ps 89: 15 we are taught: "Blessed are the people who learn to acclaim you. They walk in the light of your presence, Yahweh." In Ps 104: 2 we read about God: "He covers himself with light as with a garment." Isaiah 2: 5 encourages us: "House of Jacob, come, and let us walk in the light of Yahweh."

All these pronouncements make it clear that the Hebrew conception of God was very concrete. Just as heaven as the residence of God was seen as part of the cosmos, so God was also deemed to be an entity within the cosmos – often associated with fire, flames and light. After all, the author of the book of Job informs us in 22: 14 that God "walks on the vault of the sky" – which means that he is an entity within the cosmos as a whole, although he is also the creator of the cosmos.

We are also informed that the Israelite leader, Joshua, prayed to God to make the sun and the moon stop their progress across the sky in order to get more daylight during a battle the Israelites were on the verge of winning (Josh 10: 12–13). In other words, God was seen as having the power to stop the movements of the heavenly bodies.

The Old Testament often mentions God's eyes, ears, face, arms, hands or voice, as well as his love, anger, sorrow and disappointment – as if he had a human form and a human mind with human emotions. Biblical scholars tend to ascribe this usage to the literary construct of "anthropomorphism", the tendency to make God more intelligible by ascribing human attributes to him. These scholars also see this as figurative or metaphoric speech. It is clear in the light of all the quotations from the Old Testament that the Israelites thought of heaven as God's domicile and of God himself in physical and concrete – and even (super)human – terms.

Hebrew View of Angels

The Old Testament uses two words for angelic beings: מַלְאָךְ (*mal'ak*), which literally means a "messenger" and is mostly translated with *angel*, but we also read of *cherubs* or cherubim (Hebrew: כְּרוּבִים – *keroubim*), heavenly beings who form the entourage of God in heaven. It has already been shown that the Hebrew Scriptures identified the stars with angels (Job 38: 4–8; Ps 148: 2–3; Neh 9: 6).

The Old Testament refers numerous times to God as "Yahweh of Hosts" (for instance Ps 24: 10, Isa 54: 5, and Hos 12: 5). The word for *hosts* (צְבָאוֹת – *tsebaot*) was used of the army of angels at God's disposal, but equally to the myriads of stars shining in the sky or heaven where God lives (Gen 2: 1; Deut 4: 19; 2 Kgs 7: 16; Jer 19: 13).

It seems as if the angels were also equated with the wind and with fire. Ps 104: 4 declares of God: "He makes his messengers [angels] winds; His servants flames of fire." Ezekiel 1: 13–14 gives the following description of angels:

> "As for the likeness of the living creatures, their appearance was like burning coals of fire, like the appearance of torches: [the fire] went up and down among the living creatures; and the fire was bright, and out of the fire went forth lightning. The living creatures ran and returned as the appearance of a flash of lightning."

We are also told: "These are the four winds of the sky, which go forth from standing before the Lord of all the earth." (Zech 6: 5).

God is often referred to as "Yahweh of Hosts who sits [above] the cherubim" (1 Sam 4: 4; 2 Sam 6: 2; 2 Kgs 19: 15; Ps 80: 1). Therefore, his *hosts* or army of angels/cherubs – actually, the stars – support him. We are also told: "He rode on a cherub, and did fly; yes, he was seen on the wings of the wind" (2 Sam 22: 11).

On occasion, mortals had conversations with heavenly beings that appeared in human form. Abraham and Lot received heavenly visitors (Gen 18: 2–15; Gen 19: 1–22). Jacob wrestled with one (Gen 28: 12). Gideon was called by a heavenly being to become the leader of the Israelites (Judg 6: 11–24). An angel announced to Manoah that his son, Samson, would be dedicated to the Lord's service (Judg 13: 6–21). The prophet Ezekiel had various encounters with heavenly creatures and Daniel saw a "son of man" (Dan 7: 13; Dan 10: 16).

The way the Old Testament conceptualised of angels and cherubs demonstrates that these beings were regarded in a concrete way. They were equated with the stars, with the wind and with flames. They were not seen as "spiritual", supernatural or non-material beings; they were visible and tangible inhabitants of the same cosmos in which humans also live.

Hebrew View of Stars

The starry heavens were very visible to the people of the ancient Middle East with its clear skies at night. It is, therefore, no surprise that the Mesopotamians initiated the systematic study of the celestial bodies. It has already been pointed out that the Israelites were familiar with Mesopo-tamian star lore.

The Old Testament repeatedly stresses that God created the stars (Gen 1: 16; Gen 2: 1; 1 Sam 40: 26; Neh 9: 6; Ps 33: 6). The "hosts" of the heaven – consisting of the stars and the angels – were seen as living and intelligent beings and they had the task of singing God's praise (Ps 148: 1–4; Neh 9: 6). The reason for the creation of the bodies in the heavens was to be "lights in the expanse of sky to divide the day from the night; and let them be for signs, and for seasons, and for days and years" (Gen 1: 14). Thus, God intended them to be time keepers, as well as "signs" or warnings and omens, presumably of his intentions.

The starry skies have the function of proclaiming God's glory. Ps 19: 1–4 announces:

> "The heavens declare the glory of God. The expanse shows his handiwork. Day after day they pour forth speech, and night after night they display know-ledge. There is no speech nor language, where their voice is not heard. Their voice has gone out through all the earth, their words to the end of the world."

In other words: the heavens, with all that is contained in them, are able to speak and must, therefore, be living and intelligent beings.

According to Dan 12: 2–3, the deceased "wise" people would receive eternal life and "shall shine as the brightness of the expanse; and those who turn many to righteousness as the stars forever and ever." In other words: God's faithful could expect to become shining stars in the sky after Judgment Day.

Hebrew View of the Spirit
The Hebrew word for *spirit* is רוּחַ (*ruach*) and it has a wide range of meanings: "wind, air, breath, mind, heart, spirit". It is also used of the "Spirit of God". In the light of our finding that the Old Testament envisaged God, heaven and angels in a very concrete way, it seems likely that all these meanings of the word *spirit* were actually synonyms and that the spirit was not regarded as a non-material entity, but something composed of air or wind and equated with the breath of man. An analysis of the use of this word in the Old Testament confirms this expectation.

The whole human being is regarded as a spiritual being (Ex. 35: 21; Ezek. 18: 31). God creates the spirit within man (Zech 12: 1).

The following pronouncements in the Old Testament clearly use the words *spirit* and *breath* or *wind* as synonyms:

- "But there is a spirit in man, and the breath of the Almighty gives them understanding" (Job 32: 8).
- "Thus says God Yahweh, he who created the heavens, and stretched them forth; he who spread abroad the earth and that which comes out of it; he who gives breath to the people on it, and spirit to those who walk therein" (Isa 42: 5).
- "Then said he to me, Prophesy to the wind, prophesy, son of man, and tell the wind, Thus says the Lord Yahweh: Come from the four winds, breath, and breathe on these slain, that they may live. So I prophesied as he commanded me, and the

breath came into them, and they lived, and stood up on their feet, an exceeding great army" (Ezek 37: 9–10).
- "Woe to him who says to the wood, 'Awake!' or to the mute stone, 'Arise!' Shall this teach? Behold, it is overlaid with gold and silver, and there is no breath at all in the midst of it" (Hab 2: 19).

The human mind and heart as seat of emotions is often called spirit:

- "When my spirit was overwhelmed within me" (Ps 142: 3).
- "Therefore my spirit is overwhelmed within me" (Ps 143: 4).
- "My spirit fails" (Ps 143: 7).
- "A glad heart makes a cheerful face; but an aching heart breaks the spirit" (Prov 15: 13)
- "A cheerful heart makes good medicine, but a crushed spirit dries up the bones" (Prov 17: 22).
- "Nebuchadnezzar dreamed dreams; and his spirit was troubled, and his sleep went from him" (Dan 2: 1).

The human spirit is also seen as the seat of the mind and thoughts:

- "The spirit of my understanding answers me" (Job 20: 3).
- "My spirit diligently inquires: Will the Lord reject us forever?" (Ps 77: 6–7).

The spirit is seen as the source of desires:

"With my soul have I desired you in the night; yes, with my spirit within me will I seek you earnestly" (Is 26: 9).

The following text says that the spirit of man survives death:

"And the dust returns to the earth as it was, and the spirit returns to God who gave it" (Eccl 12: 7).

There is, though, also the idea that the spirit disappears at death:

> "His spirit departs, and he returns to the earth. In that very day, his thoughts perish" (Ps 146: 4).

From the preceding it may be concluded that the human spirit was not seen as an invisible part of man but that it often stood for the whole person, his thoughts, emotions and breath.

The Old Testament often mentions the *Spirit of God* (Gen 1: 2; Judg 3: 10; Jud 14: 6; 1 Sam 10: 10; 1 Sam 19: 23; Ps 139: 7 *etcetera*). Christians are tempted to see in these texts references to the Holy Spirit, the third Person in the divine Trinity. That was, however, never the intention of the Old Testament authors. With the expression *Spirit of God* they simply meant God himself, God who is capable of acting, thinking, talking and having emotions. The *Spirit* of God was never seen as a separate personage or entity from God. We may even translate this expression as the *breath* or *wind of God*.

Hebrew View of the Soul

In the Old Testament we repeatedly find references to the *soul* of man. The Hebrew word is נֶפֶשׁ ((*nephesh*) and it has multiple meanings: soul, self, life, creature, person, appetite, mind, living being, desire, emotion, passion, throat and breath. It could even be used for a dead body.

This word denotes the life force of a person. At the creation of man (Gen. 2: 7), God gave him his breath, his soul, his life force. At times the soul of a human is identified with his blood because when a person has lost enough blood after being wounded he cannot live any longer (Gen. 9: 4; Lev. 17: 11, 14; Deut. 12: 23).

The soul is also the seat of human emotions (Ps. 35: 9–10; 1 Sam. 20: 17; Ps. 42: 2). The soul is, however, never depicted as a "spiritual", supernatural or immaterial object. We read about a hungry soul (Ps. 107: 9) or a thirsty soul (Pr. 25: 25). The *soul* often represents the whole human being (Gen. 2: 7, Lev. 21: 1; Num. 5: 2). For this reason, many Bible translations sometimes translate the word for *soul* with *life*.

It is, therefore, safe to conclude that the Hebrew view of the soul amounted to a very concrete concept. The *soul* was not regarded as something separate from the human body; it was only the less visible aspects of the human being – his mind, his emotions, his needs and his life force as represented by his blood, even his (invisible) breath.

It is clear that the concepts of *spirit* and *soul* are somehow connected. In Isa 26: 9 they are even used as synonyms: "With my soul have I desired you in the night; yes, with my spirit within me will I seek you earnestly."

CHAPTER 3

THE EARLY CHRISTIAN VIEW OF THE COSMOS

Astrology in the Ancient Greek world
The world in which the first Christians lived differed in important respects from the Old Testament world. These Christians lived in the Roman Empire and they were ruled from Rome in Italy.

Greek became the dominant language in the countries of the eastern Mediterranean, including Greece, Asia Minor, Mesopotamia, Palestine and Egypt, due to the fact that the Macedonian king, Alexander the Great, created a vast empire within a short period of time during the fourth century BC, encompassing all these regions and absorbing the Egyptian and Persian empires. After his death, his empire was divided between his generals who became kings. This part of the civilised world became hellenised, and that is the reason why the New Testament was written in Greek. Even the educated Romans spoke Greek and that is why Paul wrote his letter to the Christians in Rome in Greek instead of in Latin – which he, as a Roman citizen, would have known (Acts 22: 25–29; Acts 23: 27).

The intellectual, religious and philosophical world around the eastern Mediterranean from the fourth century BC onwards was based on a mixture of Greek and Babylonian ideas. The Babylonian or Chaldean cosmology with its emphasis on astrology became widespread and the dominant intellectual paradigm. Taylor and Hay remark regarding the city of Alexandria in northern Egypt, the intellectual and academic centre of the world in those days, that "in this city, astral symbolism was built into its very nomenclature". They also conclude "that astrology was one of the most important 'Chaldean' cultural imports into Alexandria".[13]

Peters found: "For nearly five centuries, from the mid-second century before Christ to the triumph of Christianity, the ancient world was in the almost unchallenged grip of this half-religious, half-scientific phenomenon" of astrology.[14]

The Greeks were aware of the fact that the world is a globe and not a flat disk. Eratosthenes of Cyrene (276–194 BC) was the first person to measure the size of the earth.[15] For the Greeks, the round earth was the stationary centre of the universe and it was surrounded by the heavens containing the winds, the clouds, the planets and the fixed stars. The stars were hanging onto a huge dome or vault surrounding the earth.[16] It is doubtful, though, whether the first Christians absorbed this insight. In all probability, they adhered to the Old Testament notion of a cosmos with three stories – the heavens above, a flat earth in the middle and the netherworld below.

In addition to Chaldean astrology, the intellectual life of the hellenised world was influenced by the thoughts of Greek philosophers.

Greek Philosophers

The two most influential ancient Greek philosophers were Plato (428–348 BC) and Aristotle (384–322 BC). They based their philosophies and ideas regarding the nature of the cosmos partly on the work of their predecessors, Empedocles and Democritus.

Empedocles (490–430 BC) taught that all matter was composed of four essential ingredients or elements, namely fire, air,

---

[13] Taylor and Hay, "Astrology in Philo of Alexandria's De Vita Contemplativa", 1, 18.
[14] Peters, *The Harvest of Hellenism*, 438.
[15] Encyclopaedia Britannica, "Eratosthenes of Cyrene".
[16] Malina, *On the Genre and Message of Revelation*, 4.

water, and earth, and that nothing either comes into being or is destroyed but that things are merely transformed, depending on the shape and ratio of these basic substances to one another. The soul is, according to him, also material in nature and, therefore, indestructible. Those who have sinned must wander for thousands of seasons through many mortal bodies and be tossed from one of the four elements to another. Escape from this fate required purification.[17]

Democritus (460–370 BC) visualised space, or the Void, as a vacuum, an infinite space in which an infinite number of atoms moved that made up the physical world. These atoms are indestructible and invisible; absolutely small, so small that they cannot be divided into anything smaller. Such a particle was, therefore, called an atom (Greek: ἄτομον – *atomon*: that which cannot be cut up). Atoms differ only from each other in shape, arrangement, position, and size.[18]

Plato is remembered today especially for two intellectual constructs: the realm of ideas or forms and the division of the person into two separate substances, body and soul. The realm of ideas or forms existed in an invisible part of the universe and contained ideal "prototypes" of all attributes, qualities and essences of everything encountered in the real world. In this realm one could also find the ideal forms of virtues such as bravery, piety and friendship, of qualities such as colours and geometrical shapes, but also of material objects such as trees, animals and furniture. This realm found its unity and culmination in the Idea of the Good or the One.

The soul existed before it was united with a certain body to form a particular person. This soul pre-existed in the realm of ideas and forms and all knowledge attained throughout life amounted to recollections of the ideas or forms.[19]

---

[17] Encyclopaedia Britannica, "Empedocles".
[18] Encyclopaedia Britannica, "Atom".
[19] Barnes, "Plato".

Plato's ideas regarding the cosmos were explicated in his book, the Timaeus, and the influence of Empedocles and Democritus is clear. He wrote, for instance:

> "Wherefore also God in the beginning of creation made the body of the universe to consist of fire and earth. But two things cannot be rightly put together without a third; there must be some bond of union between them. (. . .) God placed water and air in the mean between fire and earth, and made them to have the same proportion so far as was possible (as fire is to air so is air to water, and as air is to water so is water to earth); and thus he bound and put together a visible and tangible heaven. And for these reasons, and out of such elements which are in number four, the body of the world was created, and it was harmonised by proportion, and therefore has the spirit of friendship; and having been reconciled to itself, it was indissoluble by the hand of any other than the framer."[20]

He continued that time and the heavens came into being at the same instant, patterned according to the templates of the eternal ideas or forms:

> "Such was the mind and thought of God in the creation of time. The sun and moon and five other stars, which are called the planets, were created by him in order to distinguish and preserve the numbers of time; and when he had made their several bodies, he placed them in the orbits in which the circle of the other was revolving-in seven orbits, seven stars. First, there was the moon in the orbit nearest the earth, and next the sun, in the second orbit above the earth; then came the morning star and the star sacred to Hermes [Mercury], moving in orbits which have an equal swiftness with the sun, but in an

---

[20] Plato, *Timaeus*.

opposite direction; and this is the reason why the sun and Hermes and Lucifer [Venus] overtake and are overtaken by each other."[21]

According to the Timaeus, the planets were "living creatures having bodies" whose task was to measure time. The planets, especially the sun, were composed of fire. The fixed stars "were created, to be divine and eternal animals, ever-abiding and revolving after the same manner and on the same spot…" The indestructible soul of the person "who lived well during his appointed time was to return and dwell in his native star, and there he would have a blessed and congenial existence."

For Plato, God was not a deity with personality, such as the Greek gods. He merely saw it as an embodiment of the Idea of the Good and he also calls it the Demiurge, the principle that patterned objects and entities in the world on the prototypes of the eternal ideas or forms.[22]

Aristotle did away with the teachings of his master, Plato, that there existed eternal prototypes of everything in a celestial realm. For him, every object had its own form or qualities, and these could change as time went on. An acorn, for instance, had the potential to become an oak tree.[23]

Aristotle's ideas on cosmology can be summarised as follows:

"We must explain what we mean by 'heaven' and in how many senses we use the word, in order to make clearer the object of our inquiry. In one sense, then, we call 'heaven' the substance of the extreme cir-cumference of the whole, or that natural body whose place is at the extreme circumference. We

---

[21] Plato, *Timaeus*.

[22] Barnes, "Plato".

[23] Kenny, "Aristotle".

> recognize habitually a special right to the name 'heaven' in the extremity or upper region, which we take to be the seat of all that is divine. In another sense, we use this name for the body continuous with the extreme circumference which contains the moon, the sun, and some of the stars; these we say are 'in the heaven'. In yet another sense we give the name to all body included within extreme circumference, since we habitually call the whole or totality 'the heaven'. The word, then, is used in three senses."[24]

It is clear that Aristotle's conception of the heavens more or less coincided with that of the Judeans and other ancient peoples. He also taught that the heavenly bodies are not composed of the four terrestrial elements but are made up of a superior and indestructible fifth element, the so-called "quintessence." In addition, the heavenly bodies have souls, or supernatural intellects, which guide them in their travels through the heavens.[25]

Philo of Alexandria

Philo of Alexandria (10 BC – AD 50), a hellenised Jewish theologian and philosopher and contemporary of Jesus, wrote the following regarding the cosmos in his book On the Giants:

> "Those beings, whom other philosophers call demons, Moses usually calls angels; and they are souls hovering in the air. And let no one suppose, that what is here stated is a fable, for it is necessarily true that the universe must be filled with living things in all its parts, since every one of its primary and elementary portions contains its appropriate animals and such as are consistent with its nature; – the earth containing

---

[24] Aristotle, *On the Heavens*, Liber 1: 9.
[25] Kenny, "Aristotle".

terrestrial animals, the sea and the rivers containing aquatic animals, and the fire such as are born in the fire (but it is said, that such as these last are found chiefly in Macedonia), and the heaven containing the stars: for these also are entire souls pervading the universe, being unadulterated and divine, inasmuch as they move in a circle, which is the kind of motion most akin to the mind, for every one of them is the parent mind. It is therefore necessary that the air also should be full of living beings. And these beings are invisible to us, inasmuch as the air itself is not visible to mortal sight. But it does not follow, because our sight is incapable of perceiving the forms of souls, that for that reason there are no souls in the air; but it follows of necessity that they must be comprehended by the mind, in order that like may be contemplated by like."[26]

It is clear that Philo was influenced by the Old Testament as well as the prevalent Hellenistic intellectual climate of his day. It will be shown that the authors of the various writings in the New Testament were children of their time and that they held similar views.

The early Christian biblical authors could not escape the influence of Mesopotamian astrology and Greek philosophy. They were, of course, also influenced by the Hebrew Scriptures, their only Bible in the time before the letters of Paul and the Gospels were recognized as inspired Scripture.

The early Christians lived in this world. How pervasive the influence of astrology was, is demonstrated by the fact that Paul sailed from Malta to Italy in a ship called the "Twin Gods" or the "Twin Brothers" (Acts 28: 11). In Greek the name was Διόσκουροι (*Dioskouroi*), the name of the constellation known to us as Gemini with Castor and Pollux as the principal stars.

---

[26] Philo, *On the Giants*, 6–9.

The Aristotelian worldview, as adapted by Christian theologians. Earth forms the stationary centre and is surrounded by the clouds, the orbits of the planets and the firmament upon which the fixed stars with the Zodiac were located. The description given on the outer rim of the cosmic vault reads: COELUM EMPIRIUM (sic) HABITACULUM DEI ET OMNIUM ELECTORUM (the empire of heaven, the dwelling of God and all of the elect).

The illustration (above) shows how generations of people, including Christians, after the time of Aristotle visualised the cosmos.

The Early Christian View of Heaven and Earth
The word used for *heaven* in the New Testament is οὐρανός (*ouranos*). This Greek word has a whole range of meanings: the vaulted expanse of the sky with all things visible in it, the universe, the world, the aerial heavens or sky, the region where the clouds and the tempests gather and where thunder and lightning are produced, the starry heavens, the region above the starry heavens, the seat of order

of things eternal and where God and other heavenly beings dwell. This is more or less the range of meanings as used by Aristotle.

The name Ouranos is also known in its Latin transcription, namely Uranus. This was the name of the ancient Greek god of the heaven or the sky. He ruled over the whole expanse above the earth and that means that the single word "ouranos" was applicable to all the spaces above the earth. This name was, incidently, given to a planet discovered in 1781 with the aid of a telescope.[27]

The early Christians regarded heaven in a very concrete way as the vault surrounding the earth, the whole space occupied by the winds and clouds, the stars and the home of God and the angels – just as in the Old Testament – and for them the one word for *heaven* encompassed all its various aspects. The influence of Plato, Aristotle and Philo may also be detected. Heaven is, therefore, always described as being "up there" or "above" (Mark 1: 10; John 3: 13; John 6: 38; Acts 7: 55; Acts 10: 11; Eph 4: 10; Col 3: 1–2). Paul wrote that he received visions and revelations when he was "caught up into the third heaven" and was "caught up into Paradise" (2 Cor 12: 2, 4). For him, the third heaven would have consisted of the dwelling of God himself; the second heaven being the heaven of the stars and the first heaven being the sky filled with clouds – just as the Hebrews and Aristotle regarded the heavens.

We read of various persons who saw the heavens opened and had a vision of God, Jesus or the angels. The following examples come to mind:

- Jesus, directly after his baptism (Mark 1: 10–12);
- Stephen, who was stoned to death (Acts 7: 55–56);
- Paul, on the road to Damascus (Acts 9: 3–7);
- Peter, who had a vision of a cloth lowered from the sky (Acts 10: 11–13); and

---

[27] Encyclopaedia Britannica, "Uranus".

- John of Patmos (the whole book of Revelation).

Revelation 4: 1 mentions "a door opened in heaven", through which John of Patmos could see the throne of God. That implies that the starry heaven was conceptualised as a huge dome and that God's residence was on the outer side of this dome.

John included many hymns sung by the heavenly choirs in his book. That implies that he simply must have assumed that sound could travel in the space between the stars and in God's heaven. We know, of course, that sound needs air to be transmitted and that the atmosphere of the earth extends only a few kilometres above the surface of the earth. John and his contemporaries could not have known that, of course.

When Jesus ascended bodily into heaven after his resurrection from the grave he levitated visibly skywards and it was an event that could be observed by his disciples, until he disappeared behind a cloud (Luk 24: 51; Acts 1: 9). Luke, who wrote these reports, must have likewise assumed that Jesus could still breathe when he reached the highest heaven.

Bruce Malina and Adelbert Scholtz have convincingly demonstrated that the visions which John of Patmos had of God and Jesus on the heavenly throne, as well as various angels and other heavenly beings, as described in the book of Revelation, were actually descriptions of the starry skies – planets, stars and constellations. Therefore: God and the risen Christ, together with all the other heavenly creatures, dwelled between and beyond the stars, according to John. The stars were grouped into constellations, which were seen as living entities, just as the ancient Babylonians did.[28]

That the authors of the New Testament Scriptures were influenced by the prevailing astrology appears from various texts.

---

[28] Malina, *On the Genre and Message of Revelation*; Scholtz, *The Prophecies of Revelation*.

Paul wrote (Eph 1: 20) that Jesus was raised by God from the dead and that he ascended to God's "right hand in the heavenly places". The word for "heavenly places" does not only point to God's domicile above the stars, but also the starry and cloudy heavens. According to the ancient astrology, many a mythological character or hero, such as Perseus, Hercules, Cepheus and Andromeda, was elevated to the starry skies after his or her death and became constellations.

The Jewish historian, Flavius Josephus, thought that dead heroes became stars and constellations in the sky. He declared in his book The Wars of the Jews (ca AD 78) "that those souls which are severed from their fleshly bodies in battles by the sword are received by the ether, that purest of elements[29], and joined to that company which are placed among the stars; that they become good demons, and propitious heroes, and show themselves as such to their posterity afterwards".[30]

Paul seems to think that something similar happened to Jesus Christ when he was taken up into heaven. In Phil 2: 9–10, Paul writes that Christ was exalted and that "at the name of Jesus every knee would bow, of those in heaven, those on earth, and those under the earth". It is clear that Paul inludes the stars and other heavenly beings under "those in heaven".

It seems likely that there is a reference to astrological constellations in Luke 10: 19 – "Behold, I give you authority to tread on serpents and scorpions, and over all the power of the enemy." Jesus uttered these words directly after his disciples had reported that they were able to drive out demons from people and Jesus had mentioned that he saw Satan fall from heaven like a bolt of lightning. The words quoted from Jesus may, therefore, refer to the constellations of

---

[29] A reference to Aristotle's "quintessence" – the fifth element of which the stars were supposed to be composed.
[30] Josephus, *Wars,* Liber VI (1/5).

Serpens and Scorpius, which he must have regarded as embodiments of Satan and all that is evil.

Jesus clearly thought that events on earth and in the heavens were connected and therefore he could tell his disciples that he would provide them with the keys of the kingdom of heaven and that would mean that "whatever you will bind on earth will be bound in heaven; and whatever you will loose on earth will be loosed in heaven" (Matt 16: 19; see also Matt 18: 18).

The author of the letter of Jude regarded the planets – revered by his pagan contemporaries as gods – to be evil entities and, therefore, these "wandering stars" (ἀστέρες πλανῆται – *asteres planetai*) were fated to be banished to "the blackness of darkness" (Jud 1: 13).

The second letter of Peter contains a somewhat eccentric explanation of the creation myth of the first chapter of Genesis in which the four basic elements – fire, air, water and earth – figure. The readers of this letter are reminded "that there were heavens from of old, and an earth formed out of water and amid water, by the word of God; by which means the world that then was, being overflowed with water, perished. But the heavens that now are, and the earth, by the same word have been stored up for fire, being reserved against the day of judgment and destruction of ungodly men" (2 Pet 3: 5–7). It is noteworthy that this text mentions "the heavens" in the plural (οἱ οὐρανοί – *hoi ouranoi*) – in other words: the heaven of the atmosphere, the heaven of stars and the heaven as God's dwelling. These heavens, together with the earth, were formed by God's creative word out of water and they are destined to be destroyed by fire. Three of the four Greek elements, namely fire, water and earth, are mentioned explicitly, while air is implied in the plurality of heavens.

That these four elements are meant, is clear from verse 10 in the same chapter: "But the day of the Lord will come as a thief in the night; in which the heavens [plural!] will pass away with a great noise, and the elements will be dissolved with fervent heat, and the earth and the works that are in it will be burned up." Verse 12 also mentions "the coming of the day of God, by reason of which the heavens [plural!] being on fire will be dissolved, and the elements will melt with fervent heat". The Greek word used for "element" is στοιχεῖον (*stoicheion*); this word was usually used for the four elements of the cosmos – fire, air, water and earth. A similar end for the world was foreseen by Jesus, according to Matthew: "But immediately after the oppres-sion of those days, the sun will be darkened, the moon will not give her light, the stars will fall from the sky, and the powers of the heavens will be shaken" (Matt 24: 29).

Paul seems to have been critical of the prevailing philosophy of his time:

- "So we also, when we were children, were held in bondage under the elements of the world" (Gal 4: 3).
- "But now that you have come to know God, or rather to be known by God, why do you turn back again to the weak and miserable elements, to which you desire to be in bondage all over again?" (Gal 4: 9).
- "Be careful that you don't let anyone rob you through his philosophy and vain deceit, after the tradition of men, after the elements of the world, and not after Christ" (Col 2: 8).
- "If you died with Christ from the elements of the world, why, as though living in the world, do you subject yourselves to ordinances" (Col 2: 20).

It is not quite clear what Paul regarded as "elements". It may be the notion that Christians ought not to be obsessed with worldly things composed of the four elements, but that they rather had to attach value to heavenly things that are indestructible. After all, he also wrote: "Set your mind on the things that are above, not on the things that are on the earth" (Col 3: 2).

There can be no doubt that the writings of the New Testament contain various pagan Greek views regarding the composition of the cosmos.

The Early Christian View of the Underworld and Hell
The New Testament employed more than one Greek word to name the underworld, the realm of the dead:

- Hades (Greek: ᾄδης) – *Hades* was the Greek god of the underworld and was also known as Pluto.[31] This name was also used for the grave, death or hell. In the Greek translation of the Old Testament this word was used as the equivalent of Sheol, the abode of the dead. This word was used in the New Testament in Matt 16: 18, Luke 10: 15; Luke 16: 23; Acts 2: 31, Rev 1: 18 and Rev 20: 13–14. In all these texts it may mean hell or simply the underworld where the deceased are being kept.
- The abyss (Greek: ἄβυσσος – *abyssos*) – a pit of immeasurable deepness, the destination of the dead and especially the abode of demons. In Greek mythology, it was used as a synonym for "chaos" – the condition of the world before it was ordered.[32] This word appears in the following texts: Luke 8: 30–31, Rom 10: 7, Rev 1: 18, Rev 11: 7, Rev 17: 8, and Rev 20: 1–3, 13 and it was always used of the netherworld.
- Tartarus (Greek: ταρταρος - *Tartaros*) – the name of the doleful and dark subterranean region, the deepest part of the underworld and regarded by the ancient Greeks as the abode of the most wicked dead, where they suffered punishment for their evil deeds.[33] This name is only found in 2 Pet 2: 4.

---

[31] Encyclopaedia Britannica, "Hades".
[32] Encyclopaedia Britannica, "Chaos".
[33] Encyclopaedia Britannica, "Tartarus".

- Darkness (Greek: ζόφος – *Zofos*) – the darkness or blackness of the netherworld and hell. It is used in Jud 1: 6, 13 and 2 Pet 2: 4.
- The underworld (Greek: καταχθόνιος – *katach-thonios*) – this word literally means "subterranean" and it is used in Phil 2: 10 for "those who dwell in the world below, the departed souls."
- Gehenna (Greek: γέεννα – *Geenna*). This is actually a Hebrew word that means Hell. It is the place of the future punishment call Gehenna or Gehenna of fire. This was originally the valley of Hinnom, south of Jerusalem, where the filth and dead animals of the city were cast out and burned; a fit symbol of the wicked and their future destruction. It is used in Matt 10: 28, Matt 18: 8–9, and Mark 9: 43.

It must be gathered that the authors of the Christian Scriptures thought that the netherworld was located somewhere below the surface of the (flat) earth.

The New Testament also contains the concept of *hell* where the godless sinners were to be punished for their evil deeds, which they committed while still alive on earth. In the following texts this place is pictured as a huge fire or a "pool of fire and sulfur": Matt 5: 22, Matt 13: 42, 50, Matt 18: 8, Matt 25: 41, Heb 10: 27, Jud 1: 7, Rev 19: 20, Rev 20: 10, 15, and Rev 21: 8. Hell is, though, also described as "the outer darkness; there is where the weeping and grinding of teeth will be" (Matt 8: 12; Matt 22: 13; Matt 25: 30).

That Paul thought of the cosmos as consisting of three layers has already been shown. In Phil 2: 9–10 he quoted a hymn about Christ where this cosmology also appears: "Therefore God also highly exalted him, and gave to him the name which is above every name; that at the name of Jesus every knee would bow, of those in heaven, those on earth, and those under the earth…" John of Patmos likewise wrote that "no one in heaven, or on the earth, or under the earth" was able to open the book in the hand of God (Rev 5: 3).

In contrast with this, there are also texts that suggest that the faithful and repentant sinners would enter heaven immediately after death and that evil people were to enter eternal punishment directly after having died (Luk 16: 19–31; Luk 23: 43; Acts 7: 59).

The New Testament concepts regarding the fate of the dead do seem to be rather confusing since hell and the netherworld, the realm of the dead, were seen as one and the same place; after all, the same words were used to name or describe both of them. We must remember, though, that the first Christians lived in a prescientific age and it did not matter very much to them that they sometimes held irrational, conflicting and confusing beliefs.

It is clear from the preceding that the authors of the New Testament were profoundly influenced by Greek mythology in their conception of the fate of the dead. That meant that the dead were thought to be kept in the underworld, somewhere below the surface of the earth, awaiting Judgment Day, after which the faithful would be allowed into heavenly bliss and the ungodly would suffer eternal pain in hell.

The influence of Egyptian concepts regarding the fate of the dead cannot be ruled out, either. It is well known that the ancient Egyptians embalmed the bodies of their deceased kings and other important people to prepare them for the afterlife in a heavenly realm, among the stars. The dead were supplied with copies of the "Book of the Dead", a manual to guide them through all the dangers they could expect on their travels to the afterlife, including the "weighing of the heart", a trial in which their earthly lives were judged. The big difference was that the Egyptians believed that only royalty and nobility would reach the afterlife; the souls of rest of the population would cease to exist if their bodies were not embalmed.[34] In contrast, Christians believed that all believers would inherit everlasting life after death.

---

[34] Oakes and Gahlin, *Egypt,* 390–95.

The Early Christian View of God

The New Testament authors followed the Old Testament by often linking God to fire and light. Hebr 12: 29, for instance, states outright: "Our God is a consuming fire."

The Holy Spirit is often depicted as a being that appears in fire or flames:

- "John answered them all, 'I indeed baptize you with water, but he comes who is mightier than I, the latchet of whose sandals I am not worthy to loosen. He will baptize you in the Holy Spirit and fire'" (Luk 3: 16).
- "Tongues like fire appeared and were distributed to them, and it sat on each one of them. They were all filled with the Holy Spirit…" (Acts 2: 3–4).
- "Out of the throne proceed lightnings, sounds, and thunders. There were seven lamps of fire burning before the throne, which are the seven Spirits of God" (Rev 4: 5).

We are also informed:

- "This is the message which we have heard from him and announce to you, that God is light, and in him is no darkness at all" (1 John 1: 5).
- "The city [the New Jerusalem] has no need for the sun, neither of the moon, to shine, for the very glory of God illuminated it, and its lamp is the Lamb" (Rev 21: 23).

The second coming of Christ will also be a fiery event:

"… when the Lord Jesus is revealed from heaven with his mighty angels in flaming fire…" (2 Thess 1: 7).

The exalted Christ was described as follows:

- "His head and his hair were white as white wool, like snow. His eyes were like a flame of fire" (Rev 1: 14).
- 1 Tim 6: 16 proclaims that the exalted and immortal Jesus Christ is "dwelling in unapproachable light".

In addition, we are assured:

"God is a Spirit" (John 4: 24).

It has to be reminded that Plato taught that the celestial bodies were composed of fire. It may also be argued that the authors of the New Testament books were influenced by the Greek philosophers who taught that the cosmos was composed of the four elements, fire, air, water and earth. Of these, fire was the least tangible and that may be the reason why God, Christ, and the Holy Spirit were associated with fire and light.

It must be concluded that the Biblical views of God, heaven, the netherworld and hell were influenced to such an extent by pagan notions that it is impossible to divorce the biblical ideas from certain aspects of ancient paganism.

The Early Christian View of Angels and Demons

The New Testament mentions many instances where angels appeared to humans and they are portrayed as the servants and messengers of God. After all, the Greek word for angel, ἀγγέλος (*angelos*), literally means "messenger".

That John of Patmos thought that the stars in the sky were actually angels is clear from Rev 1: 16, 20:

"He had seven stars in his right hand. (. . .) The seven stars are the angels of the seven assemblies.

The author of Hebr 1: 7 quotes Ps 104: 4 – "Of the angels he says, 'Who makes his angels winds, and his servants a flame of fire.'" This author seems to have held the belief that these celestial beings are composed of the two less solid elements, namely air or wind and fire. Something similar is encountered in Matt 28: 2 where we read of the angel who opened Jesus' grave: "His appearance was like lightning."

Not all angels were benign messengers and servants of God. We often read of evil angels, Satan and his helpers – in other words: demons. Satan and his followers rebelled against God and were, therefore, thrown out of heaven. 2 Pet 2: 4 tells us: "For if God didn't spare angels when they sinned, but cast them down to Tartarus, and committed them to pits of darkness, to be reserved to judgment." In Jud 1: 6 we are informed: "Angels who didn't keep their first domain, but deserted their own dwelling place, he has kept in everlasting bonds under darkness for the judgment of the great day."

Paul also thought that the stars and constellations were living beings and in many cases, demonic in nature. In Eph 6: 12 he warns his readers: "For our wrestling is not against flesh and blood, but against the principalities, against the powers, against the world's rulers of the darkness of this age, and against the spiritual hosts of wickedness in the heavenly places." Paul's word for "heavenly places" (ἐπουράνιος – *epouranios*) may also be translated with "sky". He envisaged these "powers" and "hosts" to be composed of invisible matter (Aristotle's "quintessence"?) since they occupied the sky above. The "rulers of darkness" can only be the stars shining at night and the constellations. The influence of Aristotle and Philo of Alexandria (directly or indirectly) cannot be ruled out.

Paul also contrasted the creation, that is composed of the elements and that is prone to decay with the permanence of eternal life with God:

> "… the creation itself also will be delivered from the bondage of decay into the liberty of the glory of the children of God. For we know that the whole creation groans and travails in pain together until now. Not only so, but ourselves also, who

have the first fruits of the Spirit, even we ourselves groan within ourselves, waiting for adoption, the redemption of our body." (Rom 8: 21–23).

Paul was certain that the evil powers in the sky or heaven would not be able to alienate believers from God's love: "For I am persuaded, that neither death, nor life, nor angels, nor principalities, nor things present, nor things to come, nor powers, nor height, nor depth, nor any other creature, will be able to separate us from the love of God, which is in Christ Jesus our Lord" (Rom 8: 38–39). The word that is translated with "principalities" (ἀρχαι – *archai*) may equally well be translated with "elements". With "height" Paul had heavenly beings in mind and with "depth" he meant everything under the earth, including the abode of the dead.

In Eph 1: 20–22 were are told that Christ, who was raised from the dead and given a place "in heavenly places" was also made head of all creation, including "all rule, and authority, and power, and dominion, and every name that is named, not only in this world, but also in that which is to come". It has already been shown that heaven was seen by the early Christians as all the spaces above earth, including the heaven of stars and God's dwelling place. These powers that were subjected to Christ, therefore, include everything in the sky, namely angels, demons, planets and constel-lations of stars. In addition, Paul foresaw that the "wisdom of God might be made known to the principalities and the powers in the heavenly places"; in other words, that all the beings in the sky will have to take note that God is in control of everything (Eph 3: 10).

We are also assured that when Jesus Christ was resurrected and ascended into heaven, "angels and authorities and powers [were] being made subject to him" (1 Pet 3: 22). In other words: he overpowered all the elements (ἀρχαι – *archai*), evil demons and astrological forces in the sky.

Paul had some or other affliction: "By reason of the exceeding greatness of the revelations, that I should not be exalted excessively, there was given to me a thorn in the flesh, a messenger (angel) of Satan to buffet me, that I should not be exalted excessively" (2 Cor 12: 7). It is clear that Paul thought that Satan used evil angels or demons to do his dirty work.

The fate of these evil angels is sealed and signed and therefore Paul could write: "Don't you know that we will judge angels?" (1 Cor 6: 3). Rev 12: 7–9 tells of a cosmic battle that took place: "There was war in the sky. Michael and his angels made war on the dragon. (. . .) The great dragon was thrown down, the old serpent, he who is called the Devil and Satan, the deceiver of the whole world. He was thrown down to the earth, and his angels were thrown down with him."

There can be no doubt that the New Testament authors were decisively influenced by the Greek mythology when they thought of angels, demons and other beings in the sky. The only difference is that where the pagans saw the planets, stars and constellations as deities, the early Christians regarded these entities to be angels, deceased saints or demons – which, in practice, amounted to pretty much the same.

The Early Christian View of Spirits
There are numerous references to *spirits* in the New Testament. The word utilised is πνεῦμα (*pneuma*). It has many meanings: a movement of air, the wind; breath; the spirit, i.e. the vital principal by which the body is animated, the rational spirit, the power by which the human being feels, thinks, decides; the soul; a spirit higher than man but lower than God, i.e. an angel; the Spirit of God; also used of demons, or evil spirits, who were conceived as inhabiting the bodies of men.

Since this single word has such a rich variety of meanings it might be argued that all the meanings are actually synonyms. That means that the early Christians – just as their Greek contemporaries, as well as the Judeans before them – regarded the wind, a person's breath and his spirit to be the same thing. Their prescientific and concrete way of thinking leaves us no other conclusion, as will be shown in the analysis that follows.

Sometimes, the *spirit* represents the whole person or his mind:

- "When Jesus had said this, he was troubled in the spirit, and testified, 'Most assuredly I tell you that one of you will betray me'" (John 13: 21).
- "Now while Paul waited for them at Athens, his spirit was provoked within him as he saw the city full of idols" (Acts: 17: 16).
- "For God is my witness, whom I serve in my spirit..." (Rom 1: 9).

The *spirit* is often seen as the life-giving force, the (invisible) breath, of a person. The following texts illustrate this idea:

- "Her [the girl who was resurrected by Jesus] spirit returned, and she rose up immediately. He [Jesus] commanded that something be given to her to eat" (Luk 8: 55).
- "Jesus, crying with a loud voice, said, 'Father, into your hands I commit my spirit!' Having said this, he breathed his last" (Luk 23: 46). [This verse may just as well be translated: "Jesus, crying with a loud voice, said, 'Father, into your hands I commit my breath!' Having said this, he breathed his last." Another way of translating it would be: "Jesus, crying with a loud voice, said, 'Father, into your hands I commit my spirit!' Having said this, he gave up the spirit".]
- When Jesus met his disciples after his resurrection he said to them: "See my hands and my feet, that it is I myself. Touch me and see, for a spirit doesn't have flesh and bones, as you see that I have" (Luk 24: 39).

- "They stoned Stephen, as he called on the Lord, saying, 'Lord Jesus, receive my spirit!'" (Acts 7: 59).
- "Then will the lawless one be revealed, whom the Lord will kill with the breath of his mouth, and bring to nothing by the brightness of his coming" (2 Thess 2: 8) [The expression "breath of his mouth" may equally be translated as "spirit of his mouth"].
- "For as the body apart from the spirit [breath?] is dead, even so faith apart from works is dead" (James 2: 26).
- "After the three and a half days, the breath of life from God entered into them, and they stood on their feet" (Rev 11: 11) [An alternative translation would be: "After the three and a half days, the *spirit* of life from God entered into them, and they stood on their feet" – which proves that the words "breath" and "spirit" were regarded as synonyms.]

These texts also contain the idea that at death a separation between spirit and body takes place – although the spirit was thought of as a rather refined type of matter, like air, wind or breath. The *spirit* was also often seen as identical with the *soul*. That means that the dualism between body and spirit or soul and the immortality of the spirit or soul, as taught by Plato, probably had an influence on the authors of the New Testament. In this, they differed from the Old Testament where a dualism between body and spirit was not to be found – except in the late book of Ecclesiastes.

The New Testament often equates the *Spirit* of God with the wind. In John 3: 8 this word is used in this double sense: "The wind blows where it wants to, and you hear its sound, but don't know where it comes from and where it is going. So is everyone who is born of the Spirit." When the Holy Spirit was poured out on Pentecost Day, "there came from the sky a sound like the rushing of a mighty wind" (Acts 2: 2). In other words: God's Spirit is associated with the wind and may even be regarded as God's breath.

There is often a contrast between *spirit* and *flesh* in the New Testament (Rom 8: 1, 4; Gal 5: 17). By *flesh* the physical body is meant, but also the sinful nature of man. *Spirit* in this sense has a connection with man's conscience and his relationship with God. Therefore, Jesus could say: "The spirit indeed is willing, but the flesh is weak" (Matt 26: 41). The influence of neo-platonic philosophers may perhaps be detected here since they taught that matter was evil and spirit was noble and that the spirit had to be rescued from the vile body at death.[35]

Paul taught in 1 Cor 15 that the faithful will be resurrected on Judgment Day with a "spiritual body" or a "celestial body" – just as Jesus Christ. He describes this body as being incorruptible and he explains the difference between this spiritual body and an earthly body by stating that celestial bodies, such as the sun, moon and stars, differ in glory and power from terrestrial bodies. In the same way, the resurrected spiritual body is totally different from the earthly human body. It seems likely that Paul was – directly or indirectly – influenced by the teaching of Aristotle that heavenly bodies were not composed of one or more of the four usual elements, but of a different indestructible fifth element, the so-called quintessence or aether, and that he applies that notion to the resurrected incorruptible bodies of the faithful with which they will be ready to enter heaven.

Paul teaches something similar in Rom 8: 21, 2 Cor 5: 1 and Phil 3: 20–21 where he states that the decaying creation and our humiliating bodies will be transformed into a state of eternal glory at the second coming of Christ, a state that cannot be compared to anything on earth.

Although Paul doesn't state it *expressis verbis*, it does seem as if he thought that the "spiritual body" or the "clestial body" with which the faithful would be resurrected on Judgment Day, could be equated with the stars shining in heaven – an idea he would have found in the

---

[35] Encyclopaedia Britannica, "Platonism".

book of Daniel (12: 2–3). After all, Paul thought of the heaven, comprised of the sky filled with clouds, stars and spirits, to be parts of the same system. According to him, the sun, moon and stars have "bodies" and he uses the same word for the "body" of a star, the "body" of a living human being and the "spiritual body" of resurrected believers, namely σῶμα (*soma*) – more or less as Philo and Josephus also taught.

Heb 1: 14 declares that *angels* are "ministering spirits, sent forth to do service for the sake of those who will inherit salvation".

Evil or unclean *spirits* or demons are often mentioned in the New Testament. These two concepts are seen as identical (Matt 8: 16; Luk 4: 33; Luk 8: 27–33; 1 Tim 4: 1; Rev 16: 13–14). All demons are, therefore, also spirits. These spirits were thought to be responsible for illness, maladies and ailments and there are numerous references to such instances in the Gospels and Acts. The reference by Jesus to "serpents and scorpions" most probably referred to astrological constellations. Jesus also informed his disciples in the same breath "that the spirits are subject to you" (Luk 10: 19–20). It is, therefore, a characteristic of these "serpents and scorpions" that they are also spirits – and they were possibly also starry constellations

The word demon (Greek: δαιμόνιον – *daimonion*) origin-ally simply meant *spirit.* It later got a negative connotation when it was used for mischievous or malevolent spirits that lured people into wrong-doing or caused harm. Therefore, the faithful are warned that "some will fall away from the faith, paying attention to seducing spirits and doctrines of demons" (1 Tim 4: 1).

The Early Christians' View of the Soul
The concept of *soul* plays an important role in the New Testament. The Greek word is ψυχή (*psyche*). It has the following meanings: breath, the vital force which animates the body and shows itself in breathing; the soul, the seat of the feelings, desires, affections, aversions; the soul regarded as a moral being designed for everlasting

life; the soul as an essence that differs from the body and is not dissolved by death.

This word is often used for the whole person:

- "Take my yoke on you, and learn from me, for I am humble and lowly in heart; and you will find rest for your souls" (Matt 11: 29).
- "I will tell my soul, 'Soul, you have many goods laid up for many years. Take your ease, eat, drink, be merry'" (Luk 12: 19).
- "Then those who gladly received his word were baptized. There were added that day about three thousand souls" (Acts 2: 41).
- "It will be, that every soul that will not listen to that prophet will be utterly destroyed from among the people" (Acts 3: 23).

The word *soul* is also used as a synonym for *life:*

> For what will it profit a man, if he will gain the whole world, and forfeit his life [soul]? Or what will a man give in exchange for his life [soul]?

Man is composed of body, soul and spirit (Matt 22: 37; 1 Thess 5: 23; Heb 4: 12). The *soul* is the part or aspect of the person that is saved through faith in Jesus Christ (Luke 12: 20; Luke 21: 19; Heb 10: 39; Heb 13: 17; Jas 1: 21; Jas 5: 20; 1 Pet 1: 9). The *soul* is also the part of man that survives death and receives life everlasting in heaven (Rev 6: 9; Rev 20: 4). It seems likely that the dualism between body and *soul*, as taught by Plato, must have influenced the early Christian authors.

There are, however, also texts that signify that more than just the *soul* will survive death. Jesus said: "Don't be afraid of those who kill the body, but are not able to kill the soul. Rather, fear him who is able to destroy both soul and body in Gehenna [hell]" (Matt 10: 28).

Jesus also thought that the dead still possessed material bodies when in hell. In Matt 18: 8–9 he taught:

> "If your hand or your foot causes you to stumble, cut it off, and cast it from you. It is better for you to enter into life maimed or crippled, rather than having two hands or two feet to be cast into the eternal fire. If your eye causes you to stumble, pluck it out, and cast it from you. It is better for you to enter into life with one eye, rather than having two eyes to be cast into the Gehenna of fire."

It may be concluded that the teaching of the New Testament regarding the *soul* is sometimes rather confusing. There are texts that contradict each other. It is clear, though, that the soul was conceptualised in a concrete manner where it was seen as representing the whole (visible) person or where it was seen as the breath and life force of a person. The soul was the part of the person that was saved by Christ and that survived death.

    These prescientific ideas held by the Jews and the early Christians are at odds with what believers believe today. And, yet, believers still believe what they read in the sacred scriptures. It will be necessry to illuminate how it came about that contemporary believers do not accept the prescientific notions of the biblical authors anymore.

CHAPTER 4

THE QUR'AN

The holy book of Islam, the Qur'an, was purportedly dictated to the prophet Mohammed by the archangel Gabriel, who memorised the words and taught them to his followers after which they were written down. In some cases, he dictated a certain passage directly to a scribe.[36]

Mohammed was active during the first part of the seventh century AD on the Arabian peninsula. He had contact with Jews and Christians and he was evidently deeply influenced by their religious ideas. The Qur'an, therefore, contains numerous allusions to biblical stories and figures, inluding Adam, Abraham, Moses and Jesus.[37]

It may be safely said the the Qur'an contains a simplified Old Testament theology. It is also not a very voluminous book, containing only 114 suras or chapters of unequal length.

The main characteristic of the Qur'an is its insistence on monotheism (2: 255) and an antagonistic attitude towards polytheism and the Christian doctrine of the Trinity.

Since Mohammed lived in a cultural backwater, the Arabian peninsula, during the so-called dark ages in Europe, it is to be expected that the teachings of the Qur'an regarding the cosmos would be less detailed and sophisticated and more naïve than those of the Hebrew Scriptures and the Christian New Testament. There are some similarities, however.

---

[36] Rodwell and Jones, *The Koran*, xix.
[37] Armstrong, *Islam*, 2–30.

The Qur'an describes heaven as a physical place above the clouds and that is where God's throne is situated (2: 210, 255; 8: 8; 11: 12;). God's throne is also described as a couch on earth with the clouds as a canopy (2: 22). It is also situated over the waters (11: 7) – presumably the source of rain water in the sky. Angels are hovering around the throne (39: 75), while they also carry the throne (69: 17).

The heavens are kept in place by invisible pillars (13: 2).

God also created seven heavens or firmaments above the earth, which are layered one above the other (2: 29; 17: 44; 23: 86; 65: 12; 67: 3; 71: 16-17). It is possible that these seven heavens can be equated with the orbits of the seven planets, although the Qur'an nowhere mentions any planets, apart from the sun and the moon. These seven heavens are, however, also characterised as "seven pathways" (23: 17), which may be interpreted as the orbits of the planets.

After death, resurrected true believers will be transported by angels to heaven (6: 61), which is described as a beautiful garden that is irrigated by a river (3: 15, 31; 7: 42). This garden is "as wide as the heavens and the earth" (3: 133). Heaven has gates or doors, which will be opened on Judgment Day by the angels for the faithful to enter (7: 40).

God is seen as the eternal, all-knowing and all-powerful creator of the world and he is composed of light (13: 2; 24: 35; 39: 69). He created the heavens and the earth in six days (11: 7) and created all living creatures from water (24: 45). He placed the sun, the moon and the constellations in the sky to act as light-bearers and time keepers (13: 2; 25: 61).

Hell, the destination of the godless unbelievers after death, is somewhere below the earth and is also called the "Abyss" (4: 121–122; 7: 41; 8: 11; 101: 9). The resurrected unbelievers are transported thither by the angels of Hell after they have died and after Judgement Day (8: 50; 10: 109; 37: 20). Satan, who refused to bow before Adam

(2: 34), was banished to Hell, although he still exerts power over the earth by tempting people (2: 36, 268). Hell is descibed as a never-ending fire (2: 167; 3: 131; 8: 14) and it is clear that the Qur'an describes it in physical terms.

On Judgment Day, believers and sinners will be resurrected: "And on the Day of Resurrection, they [the unbelievers] will be assigned to the most severe torment. God is not unaware of what you do" (2: 85; see also 2: 113 and 3: 55).

When the Qur'an mentions the word "soul" it is usually meant to denote the whole human being. On occasion, it also describes the condition of a person after death. In 3: 161 we read for instance: "Whoever acts dishonestly will bring his dishonesty on the Day of Resurrection. Then every soul will be paid in full for what it has earned, and they will not be wronged."

The concept of "spirit" is used exclusively for God, who is often called the "Holy Spirit" (2: 87; 5: 110;16: 102).

CHAPTER 5

THE CLASH OF SCIENCE AND THEOLOGY

Bruno and Galileo

Various clashes between science and theology have occurred during the last few centuries. The best known is that between the Italian mathematicians, physicists and astronomers Giordano Bruno (1548–1600) and Galileo Galilei (1564–1642) on the one hand and the Inquisition or ecclesiastical court of the Roman Catholic Church on the other hand during the sixteenth and seventeenth centuries.

Bruno taught that the universe was infinite and composed of an infinite number of worlds. He could not provide empirical evidence for his theories but his speculations make sense when modern insights are considered and he influenced scientific investigations in the centuries after his time. His ideas provoked the ire of the Inquisition because they contradicted the teachings of the Bible and Aristotle. When he refused to retract his theory, he was burnt alive on the stake on 8 February 1600.[38]

Galileo was the first to use the new invention, the telescope, to study the stars. He discovered the mountains on the moon, the phases of Venus, the moons of Jupiter, the unusual shape of Saturn (due to its rings), the fact that the Milky Way contained many more stars than those visible to the naked eye and sunspots. He wrote *Istoria e dimostrazioni intorno alle macchie solari e loro accidenti* ("History and Demonstrations Concerning Sunspots and Their Properties," or

---

[38] Aquilecchia, "Bruno, Giordano".

"Letters on Sunspots"), which appeared in 1613 and this led to a warning from the Inquisition that he should not continue defending the viewpoint of Nicolaus Copernicus (1473–1543), who argued that the earth revolved around the sun and not the other way.

Frontispiece to Galileo's *Dialogo sopra i due massimi sistemi del mondo, tolemaico e copernicano* (1632; *Dialogue Concerning the Two Chief World Systems, Ptolemaic & Copernican*). From left to right are Aristotle, Ptolemy, and Copernicus (their names are written on the hems of their robes). Ptolemy holds an astrolabe and Copernicus clasps a model of a planet orbiting the sun.

His most famous book, *Dialogo sopra i due massimi sistemi del mondo, tolemaico e copernicano* (*Dialogue Concerning the Two Chief World Systems, Ptolemaic & Copernican*), was finished in 1630, and he dedicated it to the Pope, who was a friend. Since he presented the book as a mere hypothesis he initially got the approval of the ecclesiastical censors. However, the Inquisition, the Vatican's doctrinal police, subjected Galileo to a hearing in 1633 and he was forbidden to teach his views any longer and he was put under house arrest. Galileo was rehabilitated only in 1979 when Pope John Paul II conceded that the church treated him unjustly.[39]

On 31 October 1992 the Pope addressed the Pontifical Academy of Sciences in Rome and confessed that the Inquisition was wrong in condemning Galileo. This was one of the rare occasions where the Pope admitted an error of the church.[40]

With these actions, the Pope actually repudiated the dogmas of the church of previous centuries regarding the nature of the univers and also – by implication – rejected the literal teachings of Holy Scripture itself.

Contemporary Views
Christians of the twenty-first century will find it strange to learn that the Bible actually teaches that God is composed of fire and light, that the stars are actually angels, that angels are made of matter, consisting of fire, light and wind and that when the faithful die and their souls go to heaven they will, in fact, be transformed into stars in the sky. They will also regard it as fantastic that the Bible teaches that hell is somewhere below the surface of the earth. All these ideas cannot be reconciled with anything they have learnt in school about the earth and the universe.

---

[39] Van Helden, "Galileo"; Galileo, *Dialogue Concerning the two Chief World Systems*.
[40] The New York Times, 01.11.1992.

Yet, that is what we find in the Bible, regarded by the Church as the infallible and inspired Word of God and that is the reason why the Inquisition silenced Galileo with his heretical view that the earth is not the centre of the universe.

Mesopotamian astrology played an important part in how people in the ancient world thought about the cosmos, heaven, the gods, angels, spirits and the soul. Greek philosophers also disseminated ideas that influenced people centuries after their times – including the authors of the writings of the New Testament.

The various authors of the books of the Old Testament and the New Testament could not escape the influence of these prescientific and unsophisticated intellectual constructs. They likewise thought of the cosmos as a closed system, which contained heaven as God's home and the stars and the constellations that were seen as living beings, angels or spirits, together with the earth and the netherworld where the spirits of the deceased were being kept. God and all the other celestial beings or creatures were described as being composed of fire, light or wind. The human spirit and soul were seen as material entities, made of wind or breath – or, in the case of Paul, composed of the Aristotelian quintessence after the resurrection.

In other words: there were no fundamental differences between pagan ideas about the cosmos and the ideas held by the biblical authors. The only real difference was that the pagans believed in a multiplicity of gods in the heavens, while biblical authors believed that there was only a single God, together with a number of angels, saints and demons in the sky – which boiled down to rather much of the same state of affairs.

The biblical authors cannot be blamed for holding these prescientific views. These ideas were part and parcel of the intellectual climate of their times. Since nobody in those times had access to the sophisticated methods and instruments we have at our disposal today it is totally understandable that they held these naïve views.

Biblical scholars of our age ignore these ancient descriptions of God and the cosmos and dismiss them as mere anthropomorphisms, metaphors or colourful figurative speech. They regard *God, angels,* the human *spirit* and the human *soul* as totally immaterial in nature. *Heaven*, as the dwelling of God, is regarded as something outside the visible universe, as transcendent – probably in other dimensions where space and time, as we know them, do not exist. *Hell*, likewise, cannot be deemed to be part of the visible universe and is regarded as a condition in another dimension where God is totally absent. This demytho-logizing of biblical concepts actually transforms them into something no biblical author would have recognized. When we read our contemporary ideas and convictions into certain concepts and names into the Bible we actually distort the contents of the Bible.

The ancient peoples thought that they had many indications that gods and other spiritual beings exist and influence events on earth. They had no explanation for the existence of stars, for the movements of the sun, moon and planets, for the progression of the seasons, the tides of the sea, how plants could grow from seeds, for thunder storms, earthquakes or volcanoes. They regarded eclipses of the sun and the moon and the appearance of comets as mysterious warnings from their gods. For them, all these phenomena were manifestations of divine interventions in the world. The authors of the biblical books followed these examples and they only exchanged the multiplicity of pagan gods for one God, supported by a host of angels.

Informed people of our day know how all these natural phenomena can be explained scientifically and rationally. These mysteries are no longer mysteries and we don't need supernatural entities to explain them.

Flat-Earth Theology
There are contemporary Christians, though, who take the biblical pronouncements on God and the cosmos very literarilly.

This modern revival of the idea of a flat earth was the brainchild of an American travelling lecturer and quack doctor known by the pseudonym of "Parallax". He was a certain Samuel Birley Rowbotham (1816–1884) and he called his movement "zetetic astronomy".[41]

Rowbotham, and his disciples, based their ideas on the following texts of the Bible:

- Earth is not a globe: Gen 1: 9–10; Ps 24: 1–2; Ps 86: 6; 2 Pet 3: 5;
- Earth rests on waters: Ex 20: 4; Deut 4: 18; Deut 33: 13;
- Earth is immovable and the sun is in motion: Ps 19: 4–6; Eccl 1: 5; Judg 5: 31; Josh 10: 13;
- Earth is not a planet and is the only material world: Luk 18: 29–30; Matt 12: 32;
- The sun, moon and stars are mere lights: Gen 1: 14–17; Ps 86: 7–9; Job 25: 5; Isa 30: 26; Isa 13: 10; Joel 2: 10; Dan 12: 3; and
- Heaven is above and hell is below: Deut 26: 15; Ps 52: 19; Ps 53: 2; 2 Kings 2: 11; Mark 16: 10; Luke 24: 51; Isaiah 14: 15; Prov 15: 24; Ez 31: 16–17; 2 Pet 2: 4; Rev 20: 10, 13–14.[42]

This movement is still alive today and is known as the Flat Earth Society. It even maintains a website to propagate its ideas. These notions of the flat-earth theology certainly agree with the Bible, although most contemporary Christians, who rely on the Bible for their knowledge of God and his creation, cannot subscribe to this theology.

---

[41] Garwood, *Flat Earth*, 36.
[42] Garwood, *Flat Earth*, 363–69.

The Contporary View of the Cosmos
Ever since the time of Copernicus (1473–1543) and Galileo (1564–1642) our view of the cosmos has undergone various radical changes. We now know that the stars are bodies similar to our sun, only at a far greater distance. Nowa-days, it is universally accepted within educated circles that the earth is a tiny speck of dust in a vast expanse of space in which billions of galaxies are spread out.

The explanation of the cosmology of the authors of the scriptures showed that we cannot see the Bible as a dependable and reliable source of knowledge about God and the cosmos. If we want to know who, where and what God is, the Bible with its mythological foundation cannot be studied and dissected.

The universe is about 13,7 billion years old. With our strongest optical and radio telescopes and other instruments we are able to observe most of the universe.

The observable universe is about 26 billion light years in diameter, although the universe must be bigger than that. We will, however, never be able to detect the non-observable sections of the universe because the combined speed with which the earth and those parts of the universe are receding from each other is greater than the speed of light. No light or other radiation from those parts of the universe can ever catch up with us.

The accompanying illustration (below) provides a simplified view of how we regard the cosmos today. In this cosmos, there is no place for a heaven as the dwelling place of God. Believers argue, though, that God as creator cannot be part of his creation, that he is transcendent (that means, outside the universe, perhaps in another dimension) and that he must be a spiritual, non-material, all-powerful, all-knowing and omnipresent intelligence.

That brings us back to our initial assertion: God never existed, except in the minds of believers. And then one must ask: How do people of our age ought to think about God or that which may be regarded as eternal or divine?

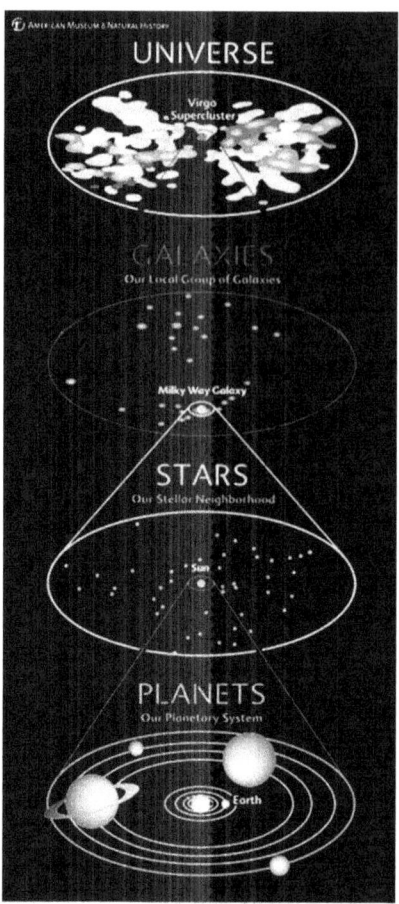

How our Solar System fits into the bigger picture of the Universe

The German theologian, Rudolf Bultmann (1884–1976), became famous for his program to "demythologize" the New Testament. By that, he proposed that Christians ought to reinterpret the mythological framework of the biblical authors and understand the message of the Bible in terms of the existentialism of Martin Heidegger.[43] This method of "demythologizing" the Bible is part and parcel of biblical hermeneutics in our day. The ancient world view, as described above,

---

[43] Perrin, "Bultmann, Rudolf (Karl)"; Van Aarde, "A Commemoration of the Legacy of Rudolf Bultmann".

is reinterpreted and the message of the Bible is presented in a manner consistent with contemporary scientific insights.

The following question, though, must be asked: where does the demythologizing of the Bible end? How far must we go to reinterpret and even remove the myths and mythical aspects of the Bible? Do we restrict that merely to the biblical cosmology, as outlined above, or do we regard all references to God, Jesus as a divine figure, angels, Judgment Day and the afterlife as myths that may be reinterpreted or even removed from the Christian faith? If we really start to demythologize the sacred scriptures, we must be consistent and take the process to its logical and ultimate end point by declaring that the scriptures, despite their beautiful aspects and the wisdom contained in them, cannot any longer be regarded as authoritative sources of reliable knowledge about the world and ourselves due to the fact that if we remove or reinterpret all the mythical aspects, very little remains.

PART B
DECONTRUCTION

CHAPTER 6

THE CONTEMPORARY VIEW OF GOD

It has been shown in the previous part that the concepts of God and other entities in creation held by Christians and Jews – and Muslims – of the present time differ widely from those held by the authors of the Hebrew Scriptures, the New Testament, the Qur'an and their original readers.

The object of this part is to demonstrate that the God who is worshipped by believers of the twenty-first century, never existed, cannot exist and is really and truly absent and gone. It will be demonstrated that it does not make sense to ask: 'Who is God?' It will be shown that God is not a 'who', a person who can communicate with us and hear our prayers. In the next part, the question will be asked: which eternal principles rule the universe? That is a question to which a rational answer is possible.

But, first of all, it will be necessary to clarify what is being meant when the word "God" is being used by contemporary theologians and believers.

Contemporary ideas about God
What do Christians – and to a certain extent Jews and Muslims as well – mean when they utter the word "God"? Dawkins gave a good explanation when he declared that this word is used "to denote a supernatural creator that is appropriate for us to worship."[44]

Benedict adds that the Bible is "the principal source of Western culture's concept of God."[45] It is, therefore, instructive to quote from

---

[44] Dawkins, *The God Delusion,* 13.
[45] Benedict, *The God Debate,* 40.

two Protestant creeds, the Belgic Confession (written in 1562 and revised in 1619) and the Heidelberg Catechism (compiled in 1563), to get a better idea of how Protestant Christians thought about God on account of what they are supposed to find in the Bible – read with more modern eyes. Non-Protestant Christians – Catholics and Orthodox Christians – will certainly agree with most of what these creeds declare about God. Students in theology from Reformed Churches who want to enter the ministry are required to declare solemnly that they accept the teachings of these creeds as a faithful rendering of "scriptural truths".

The Belgic Confession gives this definition or description of God:

> **"Article 1: The Only God**
> We all believe in our hearts and confess with our mouths that there is a single and simple spiritual being, whom we call God – eternal, incomprehensible, invisible, unchangeable, infinite, almighty; completely wise, just, and good, and the overflowing source of all good."
>
> **"Article 13: The Doctrine of God's Providence**
> "We believe that this good God, after he created all things, did not abandon them to chance or fortune but leads and governs them according to his holy will, in such a way that nothing happens in this world without his orderly arrangement.
> "Yet God is not the author of, nor can he be charged with, the sin that occurs. For his power and goodness are so great and incomprehensible that he arranges and does his work very well and justly even when the devils and wicked men act unjustly.
> "We do not wish to inquire with undue curiosity into what he does that surpasses human understanding and is beyond our ability to comprehend. But in all humility and reverence we adore the just judgments of God, which are hidden from us,

being content to be Christ's disciples, so as to learn only what he shows us in his Word, without going beyond those limits.

"This doctrine gives us unspeakable comfort since it teaches us that nothing can happen to us by chance but only by the arrangement of our gracious heavenly Father. He watches over us with fatherly care, keeping all creatures under his control, so that not one of the hairs on our heads (for they are all numbered) nor even a little bird can fall to the ground without the will of our Father."

In the Heidelberg Catechism one finds the following descriptions of God:

"**Question 26.** What believest thou when thou sayest, 'I believe in God the Father, Almighty, Maker of heaven and earth'?
Answer: That the eternal Father of our Lord Jesus Christ (who of nothing made heaven and earth, with all that is in them; who likewise upholds and governs the same by his eternal counsel and providence) is for the sake of Christ his Son, my God and my Father; on whom I rely so entirely, that I have no doubt, but he will provide me with all things necessary for soul and body and further, that he will make whatever evils he sends upon me, in this valley of tears turn out to my advantage; for he is able to do it, being Almighty God, and willing, being a faithful Father."

"**Question 27.** What dost thou mean by the providence of God?
Answer: The almighty and everywhere present power of God; whereby, as it were by his hand, he upholds and governs heaven, earth, and all creatures; so that herbs and grass, rain and drought, fruitful and barren years, meat and drink, health

and sickness, riches and poverty, yea, and all things come, not by chance, but by his fatherly hand."

"Question 28. What advantage is it to us to know that God has created, and by his providence does still uphold all things?
Answer: That we may be patient in adversity; thankful in prosperity; and that in all things, which may hereafter befall us, we place our firm trust in our faithful God and Father, that nothing shall separate us from his love; since all creatures are so in his hand, that without his will they cannot so much as move."

In other words: Christians claim that there is a perfect, omnipotent, omniscient and omnipresent spiritual being who created everything and is still in control of everything – even the bad things that happen to us. He is supposed to be totally good, wise, just, infinite, unchanging, eternal, merciful, loving and caring. Since he is the creator of the universe, he cannot be part of the universe but must exist somewhere outside of it, outside the space and time in which we exist. He is, in other words, eternal and transcendent.

It is clear the the compilers of these creeds, who were wrtten during the time of the Renaissance, stripped away most of the mythological elements in the Bible from their descriptions of God and his creation. Although they lived before the time of Galileo, they must have felt that they could not take the biblical pronouncements too literarilly and they conceived of God in a more abstract way.

This way of thinking about God is called *theism*.

It does seem as if there is not always unanimity between theists regarding their conception of God. Some find him to be so hidden and strange that it is actually impossible to say anything meaningful about him and we can only understand him by way of analogy.[46] Others,

---

[46] Springer, *Waar, Wat en Wie is God?*

though, think that we can make definitive statements about God on account of how he revealed himself in his creation and in the sacred scriptures.[47] In this book, the conception of God as defined in the sections quoted from the creeds will be used since these seem to be the ideas held by most contemporary theists and Christians.

Since the adherents of Judaism use the part of the Bible called the Old Testament by Christians, their conception of God will not differ very much from that of Christians. The Qur'an, the holy book of Islam, contains many references to events and characters in the Christian Bible and it may be assumed that the Islamic idea of God (Allah) does not depart very far from the Christian idea – apart from the doctrine of the divine Trinity. It may be safely said that Jews and Muslims may also be regarded as theists. When the Christian conception of God is analysed in this chapter, most of what will be said will also apply to these other two religions.

On account of the preceding, it is possible to name a number of characteristics attributed to God by believers:

- *Omnipotence*: Since he is the Creator of the universe and controls all events withing this universe, he must be deemed to be omnipotent. As creator, he did not only decree *that* the universe should pop into existence; he also decreed *how* everything had to be; that means that he also drew up the specifications for the universe.
- *Omnipresence*: As Creator of the universe, he cannot be part of it. Therefore, he exists outside the space in which the universe exists. Since he transcends all space it is possible for him to be invisibly present at any point in his creation.
- *Omniscience*: God knows everything there is to know, including the thoughts of every human being.

---

[47] Hyman, *A Short History of Atheism*, 47–66.

- *Eternity*: God was not created by any other agent or being and is his own reason for existence. He exists outside time that started when he created the universe and, therefore, he can oversee past, present and future.
- *Personality*: The Christian, Jewish and Muslim God is a person and has a personality and self-consciousness since he can communicate with intelligent beings, such as humans and angels. He can call Himself 'I' and 'me'. He has feelings such as love, anger, disappointment, jealousy. sorrow and compassion.
- *Goodness and perfection*: The Christian, Jewish and Muslim God, as the supreme being, is without flaws, mistakes or imperfections. In all his dealings with his creatures his actions are benevolent, caring and aimed at promoting that which is good and right.

Certain philosophers and theologians have devised other conceptions regarding God since they did not always quite agree with the theism of Christianity or Islam. These alternatives to theism must be mentioned briefly:

- *Pantheism:* This is the philosophy that teaches that there is an identity between God and the universe. Everything that exists – matter, spirit, forces, energy, laws – partakes in God's existence.
- *Panentheism:* This philosophical and theological movement declares that the universe partakes in God's existence, but that God is greater than the universe.
- *Deism:* The philosophy of deism can be described as the belief that God initially created the world but that he withdrew himself and refrains from interfering with the natural order of things.

- *Agnosticism:* Agnosticism boils down to skepticism regarding religious matters and, especially, the existence of God.
- *Atheism:* There are people who reject any belief in divine or spiritual entities and the possibility that a person can continue to exist in an afterlife after having died.

CHAPTER 7

EFFORTS TO PROVE THE EXISTENCE OF GOD

Through the centuries, there have been various attempts to prove the existence of God with rational or philosophical arguments. The rise of agnosticism and atheism since the nineteenth century prompted many theologians to seek or repeat arguments to prove that God really does exist.

The Scriptural View
The Bible does not try to prove that God exists and his existence is taken for granted. The nearest that the Bible comes to a "proof" for God's existence are the following words in Ps 19: 1–2 –

> "The heavens declare the glory of God. The expanse shows his handiwork. Day after day they pour forth speech, and night after night they display knowledge."

This is echoed by the apostle Paul:

> "For the invisible things of him [God] since the creation of the world are clearly seen, being perceived through the things that are made, even his everlasting power and divinity; that they [the unbelievers] may be without excuse" (Rom 1: 20).

In other words: the fact that the world exists, tells us that there must be a creator who has "everlasting power and divinity".

The Qur'an also regards the existence of God or Allah as self-evident. The holy book of the Muslims starts with these words:

> "In the name of Allah, Most Gracious, Most Merciful. Praise be to Allah, the Cherisher and Sustainer of the worlds; Most Gracious, Most Merciful; Master of the Day of Judgment. Thee do we worship, and Thine aid we seek."

Radio journalist, John Humphreys, attended a sermon by the well-known evangelist, Dr Billy Graham, who repeatedly quoted from the Bible to prove a point. Humphreys wrote:

> "This always puzzles me: if a preacher is using the Bible to convert someone, to prove that God exists, then surely he must first prove that the Bible is the truth and not just a collection of writings that contradict each other and were written long after the events they purport to describe. If, on the other hand, he assumes we already accept the truth of the Bible, why is he trying to convert us?"[48]

I clearly remember an incident from my youth. I was shocked when a school mate of mine declared that he didn't believe in God. Because I didn't know how to convince him of his error, I asked our minister of religion for advice. He told me to quote the following words from Ps 14:1 to this boy: "The fool has said in his heart, 'There is no God.'" I tried this approach, but the boy only laughed and said: "Who says the Bible is right?"

This incident proves that it doesn't help to quote from the Bible in an effort to convince a non-believer because he just doesn't accept anything contained in the Bible.

Karen Armstrong has clearly shown in her book, The History of God, that the Israelites did not always have a fully developed notion

---

[48] Humphreys, *In God we Doubt*, 31–32.

of who and how their God, Yahweh, was. They initially regarded him as a battle god and simply as one of a number of other gods. The Jews were only really weaned from polytheism after the Babylonian exile when the Hebrew Bible started to take shape and they heeded the calls of the prophets to worship and acknowledge only one God.[49]

Philosophical Proofs
Attempts to prove God's existence were made by Greek philosophers and were continued during the Middle Ages and into modern times. Many subsequent philosophers demonstrated conclusively that these "proofs" are flawed. Professor Antony Flew, who at one time was "the world's most notorious atheist" and who converted to theism at an advanced age, admitted, "Science qua science cannot furnish an argument for God's existence."[50] Other theists, such as Francis Collins, admit that no waterproof evidence for the existence of God can be produced; it is only possible to demonstrate the probability that he does exist.[51]

Shermer is of the opinion that those who assert that God exists have the burden of proof. If they cannot prove that God exists, then one may assume that he does not exist.[52] This point of view is in accordance with one of the axioms of jurisprudence: he who alleges, must provide the evidence.

An interesting effort to prove God's existence was proposed by the German mathmatician, Kurt Gödel, during the early part of the 20th century. He refined Saint Anselm's so-called "ontological argument" for God's existence by converting it to a mathematical theorem. This effort has received some attention in recent years when a computer scientist ran this theorem on his computer in 2013.

---

[49] Armstrong, *A History of God*; Armstrong, *The Bible*.
[50] Flew, *There is a God,* 155.
[51] Cunningham, *Decoding the Language of God,* 45.
[52] Shermer, *The Believing Brain,* 337–38.

Benzmüller and Paleo, though, demonstrated that not all mathematicians concur with this "proof" and that it cannot be regarded as universally accepted.[53]

Since all these "proofs" for the existence of God have been discredited by various thinkers it is not necessary to repeat their arguments. It suffices to say that no foolproof argument has, as yet, been presented to prove that the Jewish, Christian and Muslim God does exist. The fact that there are many atheists, agnostics and polytheists in the world is a demonstration of the fact that no convincing proof has ever been devised, otherwise everybody would have agreed that this God does, in fact, exist.

Proof Unnecessary

Adrio König, well-known Reformed theologian from South Africa, is of the opinion that the existence of God does not need to be proved since his existence is supposed to be self-evident. It will also amount to an insult to his majesty to try to prove that he exists with philosophical proofs. Instead, it befits us to accept God's power and simply worship him. He proved his own existence through his deeds in history by guiding his people, the Israelites and delivering them from slavery in Egypt and from exile in Babylonia.[54]

The trouble with this argument is that the existence of God is by no means self-evident. If that were the case, everybody would have agreed that he exists. That is, however, not the case. Therefore, it cannot be accepted that God's existence does not need to be proved. Furthermore, there is ample evidence that the biblical reports about God's purported assistance to Israel are for the most part fiction and propaganda.

---

[53] Benzmüller and Paleo, "Experiments in Computational Metaphysics".
[54] König, *Hier is Ek!* 169–79.

CHAPTER 8

ATTEMPTS TO SHOW THE IMPROBABILITY OF GOD'S EXISTENCE

God's Existence Cannot be Proved or Disproved
Richard Dawkins, a vociferous advocate of atheism, declares that – according to him – although the existence of God cannot be proved or disproved, the probability of his existence is far below 50%. He also concludes: "God almost certainly does not exist".[55] Some theists argue that the burden of proof rests on atheists to prove the non-existence of God. Until now, no such proof has been forthcoming and a stalemate seems to have developed.[56]

This is more or less the position of a number of opponents of theism. It is necessary to investigate their arguments why the existence of God is only an improbability and not an impossibility.

The Problem of Evil, Misery and Suffering
The existence of evil, misery and suffering in the world is, according to atheists, agnostics, and skeptics, incompatible with the existence of an omnipotent, omniscient and benevolent God.

Celsus, the ancient philosopher and critic of Christianity, whose work The True Word was written between 170 and 180 AD, had similar thoughts:

---

[55] Dawkins, *The God Delusion,* 158.
[56] Benedict, *The God Debate,* 72.

> "If these are his works, how is it that God created evil? And how is it that he cannot persuade and admonish (men)? And how is it that he repents on account of the ingratitude and wickedness of men? He finds fault, moreover, with his own handwork, and hates, and threatens, and destroys his own offspring. Whither can he transport them out of this world, which he himself has made?"[57]

Skeptics, atheists and agnostics point out that theistic religions cannot explain the reality of evil and suffering and they use the following arguments to bolster their position:

We are told in Genesis 1 that God created a perfectly good world. In Genesis 3 the phenomenon of evil is explained by introducing the Devil in the form of a snake who seduced the first humans to become disobedient towards God by eating the fruit of a forbidden tree.

Here one must ask: where did the Devil come from? Who created him – if he really exists? The only possible answer is that God must have created him. But – why did the Devil start a rebellion against his creator? Nobody can answer that. There can absolutely be no justification for this step and it militates against all reason.

Many Christians blame the Devil for all the pain, suffering, crime and calamities that befall us (see, for instance, the Westminster Confession, ch 1/I, ch 5/VI and ch 6/I) – as if that exonerates God. But we have to remember that God supposedly created the Devil, just as everything else in his creation. The conventional view is that Satan is a fallen angel.[58] But then one may ask: why did an omniscient God risk creating certain angels if he knew beforehand that they would rebel against him? If the Devil exists, then the blame has to be put on

---

[57] As quoted in Origen, *Contra Celsum,* Liber VI: 53.
[58] Belgic Confession, art 12.

the Creator for calling him into existence and thereby for indirectly causing all the suffering and evil in the world.[59]

Article 13 of the Belgic Confession – quoted at the beginning of this part – asserts that God created everything and still rules his creation, but that he cannot be held responsible for all the bad things happening in the world. That might perhaps be the message of the Bible, but it just does not make sense. If God really created everything, then he also created children with deformities, illnesses such as smallpox, cancer and HIV/AIDS, all sorts of noxious viruses, psychoses, and dementia. If he is the cause of everything in this world, then he is also the cause of crime, prostitution, child neglect, alcoholism, poverty, famine, malnutrition, wars and natural catastrophes such as bush fires, floods, droughts, volcanic outbursts, and earthquakes.

In contrast with the Belgic Confession, the Heidelberg Catechism describes in Q & A 27 the providence of God as "the almighty and everywhere present power of God; whereby, as it were by his hand, he upholds and governs heaven, earth, and all creatures; so that herbs and grass, rain and drought, fruitful and barren years, meat and drink, health and sickness, riches and poverty, yea, and all things come, not by chance, but by his fatherly hand." The Catechism also mentions in Q & A 26 "whatever evils he sends upon me."

The Catechism, therefore, makes it clear that natural disasters such as drought and barren years, as well as sickness, poverty, famines and other calamities don't just happen – they are sent by God. If that is the case, then he cannot be the good, loving, benevolent and caring God believers picture him to be. The terrible destruction and loss of life brought about by two world wars caused a large percentage of the people in Europe to turn their backs on Christianity and the church. They argued that there cannot be a God if he tolerated and allowed all that violence, cruelty and destruction. If he really is benevolent,

---

[59] Cunningham, *Decoding the Language of God*, 66–67.

omnipotent and omniscient, why did he not intervene and stop the carnage? After all – the Bible contains many stories about God's intervention in human affairs. Why don't we see that in our time?

One can predict with confidence that something similar will come to pass in war-torn Islamic countries, such as Syria, Iraq, Afghanistan, Yemen and Libya. People will, inevitably, start to argue that Allah seems to be powerless or unwilling to stop the wholesale slaughter and destruction and that he, therefore, probably cannot exist.

Stenger formed the following proof for God's non-existence:

> "You can prove by logical deduction that an omniscient, omnibenevolent, and omnipotent God does not exist given the gratuitous suffering in the world. By the definition of omniscience, God knows every place where there is suffering. By the definition of omnibenevolence, God does not want anything to suffer. By the definition of omnipotence, God has the capacity to undo suffering. Suffering exists, therefore an omniscient, omnibenevolent, omnipotent God does not exist."[60]

Cunningham argues as follows against the existence of God:

> "If God exists, by definition God is perfect, all good, all loving, all knowing, and all powerful.
> Such a God could not do, or permit the occurrence of, any evil or suffering to any other being.
> However, evil and suffering occur and really exist.
> Therefore, God as defined, does not exist."[61]

Cunningham also argues that God is not supposed to gamble. He supposedly wasn't taking any chances when he created the first

---

[60] Stenger, *The New Atheism*, 79.
[61] Cunningham, *Decoding the Language of God*, 58.

humans, Adam and Eve, with free will. As an omniscient God, he must have known precisely that these humans would fall into sin. He is, therefore, ultimately responsible for the fall of man.[62] It is, therefore, grossly unfair of him to grill sinners for all eternity in the flames of hell after they have died.[63]

Not only learned scientists and philosophers use the argument that the reality of pain, suffering and injustice is incompatible with the idea of a loving and caring God. Ordinary folks also think that way. The following letter (translated from Afrikaans) recently appeared in the Sunday newspaper, Rapport, in South Africa under the caption: "Ridiculous to thank God for money". A certain Len Evans wrote:

> "I refer to the news item last week regarding the millions donated for a sick child. I find it ridiculous that people thank God for the money they collected themselves. God does not care because he doesn't exist. Should he have existed, he would not have caused this child – and millions other innocent children – to become sick and suffer. Now people donate their money and thank God. Ridiculous."[64]

Some theologians tried to justify the fact that God tolerates or even causes pain and suffering by maintaining that we, humans, cannot fathom God's intentions and that he does not need to explain his actions. It is often said that God includes suffering in his providential plans for mankind in order to reach good results. Cunningham finds this unacceptable. If this God is really a good God, then it is inconceivable that he will find a good reason to let his creatures suffer.[65] Neither is it comprehensible that he will punish the vast majority of

---

[62] Cunningham, *Decoding the Language of God*, 156.
[63] Cunningham, *Decoding the Language of God*, 183.
[64] Rapport, 09.10.2016.
[65] Cunningham, *Decoding the Language of God* 62, 68.

mankind by letting them be barbecued for all eternity in the flames of hell. It cannot be fair that he allows only a small minority of sinners to enter heavenly bliss (Matt 22: 13–14; Luk 13: 23–24).[66]

God created a perfectly good world, according to Gen 1: 31, and he placed the first humans in the Garden of Eden, although he allowed his creation to be ruined by evil humans. He had, though, the power to prevent this. That he could do so, is proved by the fact that he supposedly created a perfect heaven for the relatively few souls who are to be saved. Why did he not see to it that the perfectly good world stayed that way?[67]

Keith Ward tries to circumvent the inexplicability of suffering, pain and evil by declaring: "The answer, to put it simply and bluntly, is that God cannot prevent the existence of suffering and evil." The reason for that is that God is not omnipotent – although "there is no possible power that is greater than God." He cannot do anything he pleases. If that were the case, he would be the ultimate cause of evil and suffering.[68] Since all possible universes and every possible state of affairs exist in his mind, he cannot eliminate them – although he does not necessarily agree with them.[69]

He adds that God gave human beings free will and that implies that they can choose to do evil things. "That is written into the structure of the universe, and it cannot be changed, not even by God."[70] He also puts it this way: "God cannot help creating evil, as a necessary condition or unpreventable consequence of (necessarily?) creating creatures such as human beings."[71]

---

[66] Cunningham, *Decoding the Language of God* 63–64.
[67] Cunningham, *Decoding the Language of God* 64–65.
[68] Ward, *Is Religion Irrational?* 32–33.
[69] Ward, *Is Religion Irrational?* 35.
[70] Ward, *Is Religion Irrational?* 40.
[71] Ward, *Is Religion Irrational?* 76.

Ward finds that people who suffer in this life must, somehow, be compensated for that fact and, therefore, one might suppose that there will be "a life after death, where those who have suffered greatly on earth can find in a continued existence after death some meaning for their suffering ..."[72] This argument reminds one of Karl Marx who famously wrote that religion is "the opium of the people" – a drug to lessen their suffering.

Adrio König has a similar argument. He admits that it is not possible to explain suffering and evil if one regards God to be omnipotent and loving. God is, however, not om-nipotent in the sense that he causes everything to happen. There are many role players in all events on earth – the Devil and all the people and they do things that God cannot approve of but also cannot prevent. We have the promise, though, that all evil will be eradicated on Judgment Day when the Devil's influence will be finally broken.[73]

The trouble with Ward and König is that they cannot really justify their viewpoints from the Bible. A number of biblical verses are quoted in a next chapter that declare that God can do anything, that he has immutable plans which he executes and that he directly causes bad things to happen to people. The oldest Christian creed, the Apostles' Creed, starts with these words: "I believe in God the Father, Almighty, Maker of heaven and earth." Christians have through the ages accepted that God is almighty, omnipotent, and that he created and rules everything. Ward and König actually contradict this core belief.

Most Christians will find Ward's and König's arguments unacceptable and they will find this powerless God to be a very unsatisfactory explanation for the existence of pain, suffering and evil. If all the possible universes with all their flaws, imperfections and crimes exist in God's mind – as Ward contends – then the inevitable

---

[72] Ward, *Is Religion Irrational?* 43.
[73] König, "Daar is Soveel Sinlose Lyding", 269–79.

consequence is that evil, pain, suffering, sin and ugliness is also part of God's nature. How is it then possible for Ward to declare that God is "the supreme Good"?[74]

Christian theologians through the ages grappled with the problem of how to reconcile evil with the goodness of God, but no satisfactory answer to the problem of the theodicy – the justification of God's deeds – has ever been given.[75] The only rational outcome is: God cannot exist because he seems to be totally absent from the world with its suffering, pain, evil, crime and injustice.

On the other hand, Richard Dawkins is of the opinion that the fact that natural catastrophes and disasters, such as floods and earthquakes, exist, does not disprove the existence of God – it only disproves the existence of a good or benevolent God. God can also be a nasty God, "such as the one who stalks every page of the Old Testament."[76]

Evil Committed in the Name of God

Stenger writes that the strongest case against the existence of God is the long record of evils committed throughout history in the name of religion.[77] The Old Testament, especially, provides the best example of cruelty and genocide as ordered by God. There are various passages according to which death had to be meted out to wor-shippers of idols, pagans, sinners and others who displeased God. The original inhabitants of the Promised Land had to be exterminated to make place for the Israelites.[78]

Jesus wasn't non-violent either. In some of his parables – as recorded – he tells of people who needed to be tortured due to their

---

[74] Ward, *Is Religion Irrational?* 29.
[75] Sherry, "Theodicy."
[76] Dawkins, *The God Delusion,* 108.
[77] Stenger, *The New Atheism,* 107.
[78] Stenger, *The New Atheism,* 107–10.

failure to obey or please God; Luke 12: 47–48, Luke 19: 27, and Matt 13: 41–42 come to mind.[79]

The history of mankind tells the story of man's cruelty against his fellow human beings due to religious convictions and differences. Christians have killed untold numbers of people suspected of witchcraft, heresy and impiety. Jews were persecuted because their ancestors allegedly killed Jesus. Crusades were organised against Muslims because they controlled the holy land of Palestine where Jesus had lived. Roman Catholics and Protes-tants slaughtered each other during the Eighty Years' War (1568–1648) and the Thirty Years' War (1618–1648). Until recently, they also shot at each other in Northern Ireland. Christian fundamen-talists killed medical personnel at abortion clinics in America.

Muslim fundamentalists regularly blow themselves up in busy bazaars, busses and streets to kill as many "infidels" as possible. Suni Muslims and Shiite Muslims fight each other with tooth and claw. Hideous acts of terrorism were committed by Muslim fundamentalists in the Middle East, the Indian subcontinent, America, and Europe.

It is punishable by death in Saudi Arabia to propagate any other religion than Islam.

Recently, a story appeared on the internet about a Muslim father whose daughter was drowning in the sea. He refused that life guards rescue her since it would have been dishonourable for strange men to touch her. He was later arrested for manslaughter.

The rationalist of the eighteenth century, Thomas Paine reminds us:

> "Some Christians pretend that Christianity was not established by the sword; but of what period of time do they speak? It was impossible that twelve men could begin with the sword: they had not the power; but no sooner were the professors of

---

[79] Stenger, *The New Atheism*, 110–11.

Christianity sufficiently powerful to employ the sword than they did so, and the stake and faggot too; and Mahomet could not do it sooner."[80]

One must wonder: what type of God inspired people to commit all these despicable, violent, and cruel acts?

Meaning of the Universe and of Life
It is often asserted that life – and also the universe – must be without meaning and be pointless if there is no God. It has to be granted: science has never been able to discover whether the universe has any meaning. One may even ask: why does the universe bother to exist at all? Why is there something instead of nothing? But no answers to these questions are possible.

People who believe in God are usually of the opinion that God created the universe to glorify himself and that that is the meaning of everything that exists. The universe, though, shows no signs of that. Paul Davies wrote that people want to know why there is a universe and why is the universe the way it is. "Science is good at telling us how, but not so good on the why. Maybe there isn't a why."[81]

The life of an individual human being can be very meaningful, even if we don't know whether the universe's existence has any meaning. When that person dedicates his or her life to meaningful actions by doing good and doing the right thing, by realising valuable principles, by avoiding and resisting that which is wrong and bad, then that life can certainly be deemed to be meaningful.

A life can be meaningful when that person has pursued justice, acted rationally, helped to educate his or her fellow human beings, giving aid to the victims of suffering and illness and helped the world to get rid of harmful and noxious superstitions.

---

[80] Paine, *The Age of Reason,* 143.
[81] Davies, "What Happened Before the Big Bang?" 35.

Therefore, if the universe has no meaning that we can discover, then it seems improbable that it does have a creator.

Does God Need our Worship?
Cunningham points out that a perfect being, such as God – if he exists – by definition does not need anything. He must be totally self-sufficient. It is, therefore, unintelligible why he purportedly demanded animal sacrifices from the Israelites and required of them to keep his laws regarding various religious rituals, such as keeping the Sabbath or circumcising new-born boys. It is, likewise, strange that he supposedly expects of Christians to pray to him, to love him, to praise him with their hymns and to conduct all sorts of rituals and ceremonies to honour him, such as baptising people or celebrating the Eucharist. We may even ask: does he – if he does exist – in any way take note of the actions of puny human beings on a small planet in an insignificant galaxy in the huge universe?[82]

---

[82] Cunningham, *Decoding the Language of God,* 105.

CHAPTER 9

A GOD UNWORTHY OF WORSHIP

A Good God?
The Christian God is traditionally seen as a loving, caring, benevolent and forgiving God. Article 1 of the Belgic Confession states that he is "completely wise, just, and good, and the overflowing source of all good."

But is that what the Bible really tells us? Richard Dawkins remarked:

> "The God of the Old Testament is arguably the most unpleasant character in all fiction: jealous and proud of it, a petty, unjust, unforgiving control-freak; a vindictive, bloodthirsty ethnic cleanser; a miso-gynic, homophobic, racist, infanticidal, genocidal, capriciously malevolent bully."[83]

That is rather a mouthful. But is it true? It will be worthwhile to inspect the Bible in this regard:

Gods Sends Misfortune
The Bible tells us clearly that all the bad things, calamities and misfortune that befall us come from God:

- "Then the Lord your God will make your punishment, and the punishment of your seed, a thing to be wondered at; great punishments and cruel diseases stretching on through long years" (Deut 28: 59).

---
[83] Dawkins, *The God Delusion*, 31.

- "Joshua said, 'Hereby you shall know that the living God is among you, and that he will without fail drive out from before you the Canaanite, and the Hittite, and the Hivite, and the Perizzite, and the Girgashite, and the Amorite, and the Jebusite'" (Josh 3: 10).
- "The Lord is the giver of death and life: sending men down to the underworld and lifting them up. The Lord gives wealth and takes a man's goods from him: crushing men down and again lifting them up" (1 Sam 2: 6–7).
- "But [you] have gone in the way of the kings of Israel, and have made Judah and the people of Jerusalem go after false gods, as the family of Ahab did: and because you have put to death your father's sons, your brothers, who were better than yourself: Now, truly, the Lord will send a great destruction on your people and your children and your wives and everything which is yours" (2 Chr 21: 13–14).
- "Shall we receive good at the hand of God, and shall we not receive evil?" (Job 2: 10).
- "Doesn`t evil and good come out of the mouth of the Most High?" (Lam 3: 38).
- "I am the giver of light and the maker of the dark; causing blessing, and sending troubles; I am the Lord, who does all these things" (Isa 45: 7).
- "Shall evil befall a city, and the Lord has not done it?" (Amos 3: 6).
- "Those who had no food he [God] made full of good things; the men of wealth he sent away with nothing in their hands" (Luke 1: 53).

When reading these texts, one is compelled to ask: is this really the good, caring, and benevolent God who is being worshipped by Jews and Christians (and Muslims) of whom we read in the Bible?

In the well-known Lord's prayer, the following sentence occurs: "And lead us not into temptation, but deliver us from evil" (Matt 6: 13). That means that the person who prays is actually begging God not to subject him to all sorts of temptations. In other words: temptations in life are actually being sent by God; he causes these temptations to occur. When we succumb to temptations and commit some or other sin, then it is because God caused us to be tempted. No reason can be guessed why God would like to place his children in a position where they are overwhelmed by temptations. Does he perhaps wish them to fall for these temptations and continue doing wrong and bad things? If this is how the Bible presents the supreme being, then we can only say that that God is unfair, malicious, mean, cruel, and sadistic. He is certainly not worthy of our worship.

Divinely Sanctioned Genocide
In the book of Genesis we are told that God drowned all the people of the world through a flood because of their wickedness – except for Noah and his family. Noah was the only man to find favour in the eyes of God, but he also proved to be a disappointment by making a fool of himself by getting drunk and lying around naked after the flood had subsided (Gen 6–8). It is a legitimate question: if God is really omniscient he must have known that mankind would turn out to be wicked. Why did he even bother to create people and then be sorry about it later?

We are also reminded of God who commanded the Israelites to exterminate all inhabitants of the Promised Land, due to the fact that they were worshipping pagan gods (Num 21: 2–3; Num 33: 52; Deut 7: 1–4; Deut 20: 16–18; Josh 9: 24). This resulted in genocide or ethnic cleansing with the utmost cruelty. We read for instance: "They utterly destroyed all that was in the city, both man and woman, both young and old, and ox, and sheep, and donkey, with the edge of the sword" (Josh 6: 21). In Judg 9: 49 it is reported:

"So all the people got branches, every man cutting down a branch, and they went with Abimelech at their head and, massing the branches against the inner room, put fire to the room over them; so all those who were in the tower of Shechem, about a thousand men and women, were burned to death with it."

Punishing Innocent People
In the Ten Commandments, in Ex 20: 5, God reminds us:

"I, Yahweh your God, am a jealous God, visiting the iniquity of the fathers on the children, on the third and on the fourth generation of those who hate me."

Is this a God of justice who is speaking? Is it fair to punish children and grand-children for the wrongdoings of their parents and grandparents? Is jealousy an admirable characteristic? Something similar is given in Deut 23: 2 –

"One whose father and mother are not married may not come into the meeting of the Lord's people, or any of his family to the tenth generation."

Is this fair? How can one blame the offspring of unmarried couples and punish them for the mistakes of their parents or grandparents? They are in no way responsible for the fact that they were born out of wedlock. Why punish their descendants for centuries afterwards? They are equally innocent.

We read in the Bible of various horrible things done by God to innocent people – apart from those already mentioned. Here are a few examples:

- God required of Abraham to sacrifice his son Isaac, just to prove his loyalty – although God relented at the last moment by providing a miraculous sacrificial ram instead of Isaac. One may wonder how much traumatic terror must have gone through the mind of poor Isaac when he was bound by his own father and almost had his throat slit. This act must be regarded as a case of serious child abuse (Gen 22: 2–13). One may also wonder: why was it necessary to test Abraham's loyalty if the omni-scient God must have known how Abraham felt about his God in any case?

- God destroyed the whole towns of Sodom and Gomorrah, due to the wickedness of some inhabitants; only Lot and his two daughters were saved. Lot and his daughters did not prove to be morally upright people, either – Lot offered his daughters to the rabble when they wanted to gang-rape and sodomise his two heavenly guests before the calamity struck. His daughters committed incest with him after they had fled the destruction of their city and had hidden in a cave. One must ask: why on earth did an omniscient God decide to save Lot and his daughters if they were no better than the evil people of Sodom and Gomorrah?
- God killed all the first-born sons throughout the whole of Egypt, just to teach Pharaoh a lesson (Exod 12: 29–30); can anybody say that this was in any way a sign of God's purported goodness?
- God sent ten plagues upon the Egyptians is order to convince Pharaoh that he ought to free the Hebrew slaves. We nevertheless read: "And the Lord said to Moses, 'When you go back to Egypt, see that you do before Pharaoh all the wonders which I have given you power to do: but I will make his heart hard and he will not let the people go'" (Exod: 4: 21). In other words: God would cause Pharaoh to become stubborn so that he could punish him. Is there any fairness or justice in this?

- When Moses came down from the mountain where he had received the Ten Commandments, he found that the Israelites had made a golden calf (more likely, an Egyptian bull) to worship. Moses thereupon requested the Levites to kill people without discrimination with the sword and 3 000 adults and children perished. Aaron, Moses' brother, who did the actual work on the golden calf, though, was spared. The Levites were rewarded for their wholescale slaughter by being elevated to become a special caste, dedicated to the service of God (Exod 32).
- God sent two bears to kill 42 children because they made fun of the prophet Elisha (2 Kgs 2: 23–24); is this punishment in accordance with the crime?
- God killed 70 000 people in Israel through a pestilence, simply because David angered him by organizing a census (1 Chr 21: 14). A census, as such, does not seem to be such a bad thing, because we read in Num 1–2 of a census of the Israelites after they were freed from Egypt; why punish David and his people for doing the same thing?
- God promised to destroy King Jehoram's whole family because he did not serve God properly (2 Chr 21: 14–15).
- God allowed misfortune to descend upon a pious and upright man, Job. He lost all his belongings, his children, his health and the emotional support of his wife. God allowed all this, just to prove a point to Satan. One may also wonder: if God is really the highest authority and ruler of the universe, why did he bother to prove a point to Satan?

All these examples must force one to conclude that the God of the Bible is a capricious, jealous and sadistic tyrant – not the loving and benevolent being of whom children learn in Sunday school.

Richard Dawkins points out that most Christians nowadays cannot condone all the cruel and murderous acts listed above because it clashes with their moral standards. That proves that the morality espoused by contemporary Christians does not come from the Bible, but is based upon an inherent moral instinct, characteristic of most human beings.[84]

Sick Morality

It seems that the biblical God has, at times, a sick sense of morality.

People who do not worship this God properly and correctly are constantly threatened with everlasting punishment and pain in hell – even if they led exemplary lives in other respects. Is this punishment in any way correlated to or in accordance with the seriousness of their crimes?

God forbade Israelite men to have sex with their wives while they were menstruating, since the wives were deemed to be impure during that period. Should they be caught they could be banished from Israel (Lev 18: 19; Lev 20: 18). This is barbaric; consensual sex within marriage is nowadays regarded as a totally private matter, even when it is that time of the month.

Adultery was punishable by death (Lev 20: 10). In our time, adultery is definitely frowned upon, but it is definitely not deemed to be a capital crime. Using God's name in vain was, likewise, followed by the death penalty (Exod 20: 7; Lev 24: 16). It is certainly not polite in our time to use God's name in vain, but there is no law in most countries against it. Another crime in ancient Israel that carried the death penalty was doing work on the Sabbath (Exod 31: 15). Although Christians don't keep Saturdays as the Sabbath anymore, they nevertheless regard Sunday as the Lord's Day. However, nowadays there are few Christians who do not perform all sorts of work on a Sunday, including preparing meals, without feeling guilty in the least.

---

[84] Dawkins, *The God Delusion,* 246–47.

After God had struck the pious Job with a series of disasters and misfortunes and he and his friends had a long discussion in which God's righteousness was debated, God answered Job through a storm:

> "Now brace yourself like a man. I will question you, and you will answer me. Will you even annul my judgment? Will you condemn me, that you may be justified?" (Job 40: 7–8).

It is as if God is telling poor Job that, since he is God, he can do whatever he likes and no mortal has the right to judge him – even if he acts cruelly, unfairly, and unjustly.

We are told in Acts 5: 1–10 of a couple, Ananias and Sapphira, who lied about the sale of a property. They told the apostles that they had given all the proceeds of the sale to the church, although they secretly kept some of the money for themselves. God punished both of them on the spot for lying by causing them to drop dead – even if they were entitled to keep some of the money. One can only wonder: why did God pick on this couple? Why doesn't he punish all liars in the same way?

Homosexuality
Many people feel uncomfortable when the topic of homosexuality is mentioned or when they meet practicing gay people. It is generally accepted, though, that homosexual people cannot help their condition – they are simply born that way. It is not a matter of choice. One simply discovers that one has a sexual orientation that differs from that of most other people.

Homosexuality is not regarded as a psychological disorder anymore. The DSM-5 (2013) of the American Psychiatric Association, the handbook covering all known psychological and psychiatric disorders, does not list homosexuality as deviant behaviour or as a disorder. There is, therefore, also no "cure" for being gay.

The South African Constitution of 1996 explicitly forbids in section 9 any discrimination against people on account of their sexual orientation. The Universal Decla-ration of Human Rights stresses in articles 1 and 2 that all human beings are equal and nobody ought to be discriminated against due to any attribute he may have – and that certainly includes sexual orientation.

These insights did not exist in biblical times. Homosexual tendencies or behaviour was condemned in the strongest terms and it carried the death penalty (Lev 18: 22; Lev 20: 13; 1 Kgs 14: 24; Rom 1: 24–27). One can expect though, that an omniscient God, who supposedly inspired the Bible, had to be aware of all the findings and insights of our day and must have taken them into account when inspiring and guiding the biblical authors, but that certainly did not happen. If God really was an omniscient and caring God, these passages would never have appeared in the Bible.

Conclusion

Christians mostly shut their eyes or switch their attention off when reading the parts of Scripture quoted above. They just cannot accept that God can be jealous, cruel, vindictive, unjust, mean, unfair, murderous, and unforgiving. But one cannot come to any other conclusion when all these biblical pronouncements are being investigated honestly and with an open mind.

Is the biblical God worthy of veneration and worship? If one takes into consideration everything the Bible tells us about him, then the answer must definitely be "No" – that is to say, if he really exists. The question then has to be asked: are there any waterproof arguments against the existence of this God?

CHAPTER 10

THE IMPOSSIBILITY THAT GOD EVER EXISTED

Rational arguments

In this chapter, it will be demonstrated that there is no possibility that the God or supreme being, who is being worshipped by Jewish, Christian or Muslim believers, ever existed and that he is totally absent, gone. There are a number of rational arguments to demonstrate his non-existence without the slightest doubt.

It has been mentioned above that some of the authors who were quoted and who have dealt with this subject are of the opinion that the existence of God cannot be proved – just as his existence cannot be disproved either; one can only, at most, demonstrate that his existence is less probable than his non-existence. This viewpoint does not hold water and some original arguments will be presented here to prove without doubt that it is utterly impossible that a supreme intelligent being, who supposedly created everything and still controls his creation, can exist. It is possible to contribute some new – and irrefutable – arguments. Atheists, skeptics, rationalists and nonbelievers are able to meet the challenge of theists with these new arguments to prove that this God could never have existed.

Victor Stenger believes that those who tried to prove the existence of God could not do it beyond any reasonable doubt. He is convinced, though, that science has demonstrated undoubtedly that God does not exist, since science has utterly failed to find anything pointing to his existence. If God really intervened in the world, he must have violated his own laws of nature in order to achieve his goals. Nobody has ever observed the violation or suspen-sion of any law of nature.[85]

It has to be pointed out that absence of evidence does not necessarily amount to evidence of absence. If no proof for the existence of God could have been found, then that does not necessarily mean that his non-existence has been demonstrated.

Grayling remarks that people of our age will find it ridiculous for anybody to still believe in the gods of ancient Egypt or Greece. In this sense, we are all atheists. The question then arises: if we find it impossible to believe in these ancient gods, why do we still believe in the ancient God of the Israelites? Is there any difference between him and those other ancient gods?[86] This argument sounds convincing, but it is not a totally waterproof argument either. Christians will counter that there is a profound difference for them between the God of the Bible and the old pagan deities.

However, there are rational and foolproof arguments to demonstrate that God never existed and that the very idea of an almighty creator and ruler of the universe contains inner contradictions. These arguments are to be presented on the pages that follow.

The Axioms of Mathematics, Logics, Human Rights, Governance, and Natural Justice

The first argument against the existence of an omnipotent and omniscient supreme being, usually called God, amounts to the following: When he supposedly created the universe, God was not able to formulate the axioms of mathematics, logics, human rights and natural justice in any other fashion than we know them today. If he was the author of these axioms, it goes without saying that he wasn't able to give them any other content than they do have. That means that

---

[85] Stenger, *The New Atheism,* 81–83.
[86] Grayling, *The God Argument,* 32–33.

he cannot be the omnipotent and supreme authority since he was bound by these axioms or rules and was powerless to escape their validity.

The Encyclopaedia Britannica provides this definition of an *axiom*: "An indemonstrable first principle, rule, or maxim, that has found general acceptance." A dictionary has the following definition: "A generally accepted or self-evident truth."[87]

The word "axiom" is the English version of the Greek word ἀξίωμα (*axioma*). It is derived from the verb ἀξιόω (*axioo*), which means "to consider worthy or deserving (of belief)".

It, therefore, seems justified to propose: it is an axiom that there are axioms. Axioms must necessarily also be true in any other corner of the universe, as well as outside our universe – that is, if other universes do exist.

All the sciences taught at universities (except for theology) make use of *mathematics*. The physical sciences and disciplines, such as physics, astronomy, geology and engineering, make use of mathematical models. The laws of these sciences are written in the form of mathematical formulae. The biological and social sciences make use of statistics, the branch of mathematics dealing with probabilities, tendencies, correlations and causative factors.

Mathematics, therefore, is used to describe the formal structure or make-up of the material or physical world, as well as the living and the social world.

The whole discipline or system of mathematics rests upon a number of axioms, unprovable yet self-evident truths, which are accepted by all informed people. The best-known example of such mathematical axioms is the theorems of Euclid, the ancient Greek mathematician, with which he established the discipline or system of geometry on a flat plane.[88]

---

[87] Reader's Digest, "Axiom".
[88] Shaw, *Logic and its Limits*, 18–19; Ellenberg, *Shape*, 3.

Wells wrote: "The mathematics community by and large has agreed upon a set of axioms (today, the axioms of 'axiomatic set theory') and they use these, implicitly or explicitly, in doing mathematics. (. . .) Mathematics is the art – and, I will say, the *science* – of proving theorems, and a theorem is a statement that, given the premises laid down by the axioms and certain agreed-upon rules of inference, is apodictically true."[89]

According to Johnson, Einstein believed "that the universe is comprehensible, that it can be explained with precise mathematical laws (the simpler the better), and that the laws prevailing in the vicinity of earth are the same throughout the cosmos...." Einstein, who regarded himself as "a deeply religious nonbeliever", also regarded the word 'God' to be a synonym for the natural laws as discovered by science. "We live in a universe governed by a deep mathematical order, Einstein maintained, not the whims of a personal creator – and we may just be smart enough to figure some of it out."[90]

Paul Davies also declared: "The natural world is not just any old concoction of entities and forces, but a marvelous ingenious and unified mathematical scheme."[91]

Keith Ward wrote: "Many philosophers and mathema-ticians hold that mathematical truths are necessary: they just could not be other than they are."[92]

Antony Flew – the atheist turned theist – concurs with the physicist, Paul A.M. Dirac, who observed that "God is a mathematician of a very high order and He used advanced mathematics in constructing the universe."[93]

---

[89] Wells, "Mathematics", 21–27.
[90] Johnson, "Worshipping in Einstein's Church", 268, 275.
[91] Davies, "Is there need for a divine designer?" 280.
[92] Ward, *Is Religion Irrational?* 23.
[93] Flew, *There is a God,* 105–06.

The quoted sentences all imply that God didn't invent mathematics, he only discovered and applied it – if he is the creator of the universe. In other words: God is powerless to change the axioms and rules of mathematics.

Bertrand Russel had a similar argument. Instead of axioms, he used natural laws. He asked why God – if he exists – issued the natural laws that are in operation and not any others. If there is any good reason why these laws exist then it means that God is himself subject to law and, therefore, one cannot introduce God as an explanation for the way the universe is constructed.[94]

The discipline of *logics*, likewise, rests upon a number of axioms, unprovable yet self-evident truths, which are accepted by all informed people. Aristotle was the first philosopher to discover and formulate certain axioms or rules of logics. All information, to be accurate and true, must conform to the rules of logics and these rules or axioms describe the formal structure of truth or reliable information.

If some or other logical rule is broken when people are communicating with each other, then that communi-cation cannot be reliable or credible. If a witness in court contradicts himself and thereby breaks one of the most fundamental rules of logics, namely that two contradictory statements cannot both be true, then his testimony becomes suspect or even worthless.

There is a branch of logics dealing with commands. Instructions given to people and computers must conform to certain logical rules – otherwise these instructions cannot be carried out. A most basic rule is that two simultaneous and conflicting commands cannot both be obeyed or executed.

Even God is subject to the rules of logics. Flew wrote: "You cannot limit the possibilities of omnipotence [of God] except to

---

[94] Benedict, *The God Debate*, 161.

produce the logically impossible."[95] In other words: even Flew must have been convinced that God is subject to the rules of logics and that he is powerless to change them. That means that he – should he exist – only discovered the eternal and universally accepted axioms of logics when creating the universe; he did not create or formulate these rules or axioms.

The whole system of *jurisprudence* of all civilised countries rests on the *rules of natural justice*, another set of rational axioms. These axioms are so well known that laymen regularly refer to them. These rules amount to the following:

- The testimonies and arguments of all parties in every case or dispute have to be heard (Latin: *audi et alteram partem*); this is the principle of fairness;
- Nobody can act as his own judge in a legal dispute (Latin: *nemo iudex in sua causa*); that means that presiding officers must be totally impartial and independent when hearing cases;
- Presiding officers must apply their minds when hearing cases and deliver rational judgments;
- An accused is presumed to be innocent, until proven guilty;
- He who alleges or asserts must provide proof or evidence for his allegation or assertion;
- Nobody can be punished if he cannot be held accountable for his actions;
- Punishment must be in accordance with the severity of the crime;
- No one shall be held guilty of any offence on account of any act or omission which did not constitute an offence at the time when it was committed; and

---

[95] Flew, *There is a God*, 157.

- Agreements and contracts must be honoured (Latin: *pacta servanda sunt*).

It may be argued that *basic human rights* also rest on universal principles or axioms. The Universal Declaration of Human Rights, adopted in 1948 by the United Nations, lays down in article 1:

> "All human beings are born free and equal in dignity and rights."

The South African Constitution of 1996 declares in sections 1 and 5 that this country as a democratic state is founded on the values of human dignity, equality of all people and freedom – the same values as mentioned in article 1 of the Universal Declaration of Human Rights.

The Constitution of the Federal Republic of Germany provides for the same values of human dignity, equality and freedom in sections 1–3. The Bill of Rights in the Constitution of the United States of America deals primarily with the freedoms and equality of its citizens, but the value of human dignity is implied.

It may be accepted as yet another axiom that countries, societies and any other groups of people have to be *ruled, organized, or managed* to prevent chaos and anarchy. To achieve that, laws, regulations, and rules are needed. These laws, regulations, and rules have to compel people to behave in a certain manner – for instance, obey traffic rules – or to desist from certain behaviours, such as theft, assault *etcetera*.

Another axiom is that the *government* of any country, state, province or town has to be divided into three branches, which support each other, but which also serve to prevent a monopoly on power or the abuse of power:

- The legislative branch, which is responsible for drawing up of all the laws, regulations, and rules that have to apply in the territory over which it has jurisdiction;
- An executive branch, consisting of officials who have to execute the laws, regulations, and rules of the legislative branch; and
- An independent judicial branch, encompassing the courts of law and the Police, which have to deal with those who disobey these laws, regulations, and rules.

We know absolutely nothing about the conditions on other planets in the wide universe where intelligent and self-conscious beings may reside. We, therefore, don't know anything about their judicial and legal systems and whether they have a system of rights for their (intelligent) inhabitants. It is not so farfetched, though, to imagine that the inhabitants of these planets may have a similar set of values on which their systems of jurisprudence, government, and rights rest. We may, therefore, conclude that the principles and systems as recognised on earth, have the status of a set of universal axioms.

The important questions to be asked are these: Is there any possibility that all these axioms can be any other than what they are? Is it, for instance, in any way possible to imagine that the rules of logics or the rules of natural justice can ever be amended or changed? Since they are axioms, self-evident eternal truths or principles, they must apply always and everywhere throughout the universe. Whenever there are intelligent beings on other planets in other galaxies it is inconceivable and impossible that the axioms of their mathematics, logics, "human" rights, government, and rules of natural justice will in any fundamental manner be different from ours, just as mathematics, logics and the basic rules of jurisprudence are the same in America, Argentina, Belgium, Botswana, Canada, and Croatia.

From the preceding it must be clear that any supreme being, should he exist, must be subject to all these axioms. He cannot really be the author of these axioms and rules because they are immutable, universal, eternal and valid in all conceivable situations. Should anybody venture to argue that God did, in fact, formulate these axioms and rules, one can simply ask: did this God have any choice whatsoever in the matter? The answer must be a definite "No". There is just no way in which he could have given us any other mathematical, logical, and legal axioms or rules.

If God is subject to these axioms and rules and if he had no choice in their formulation, then he cannot be the supreme being. These axioms and rules also apply to him, should he exist, and he is powerless to change them in any way. He just cannot, in other words, be the highest authority in the universe.

Ergo: it is impossible that God exists because he cannot be the supreme authority in the universe, since he – if he does exist – must be subject to the eternal and universal axioms of mathematics, logics, human rights and jurisprudence.

The Laws of Chemistry
The science of chemistry may be defined as "the science that deals with the properties, composition, and structure of substances (defined as elements and compounds), the transformations they undergo, and the energy that is released or absorbed during these processes."[96] Every chemist will affirm that the properties of elements and compounds always stay the same when external conditions stay the same.

This fact makes life possible. Every living being is a complex chemical factory in which its organs transform chemical compounds, absorbed from nutrients, into the building blocks of its cells or other useful compounds, such as neurotransmitters, enzymes and hormones.

---

[96] Rocke, "Chemistry".

The properties of elements and chemical compounds are determined by their structures, the way their atoms are linked and combined.

We may ask: did God formulate the laws of chemistry? If so, did he have any choice in determining that two atoms of hydrogen can combine with one atom of oxygen to produce anything but a molecule of water? Did God have the power to determine that a combination of one atom of sodium and one atom of chlorine can produce anything but a molecule of table salt? Can God prevent a lump of carbon of turning into a diamond when subjected to high enough pressures? If he is regarded as the creator of the laws of chemistry then it must also be conceded that he actually had no choice in the matter and no control over the outcomes of all the different chemical reactions possible in the universe.

We may ask: is it in any way conceivable that God could have formulated the laws that regulate the behaviour and properties of all the chemical elements and their compounds in any other manner? The answer must inevitably be: "No".

Ergo: Since God is powerless to change the laws that determine the behaviour and properties of all the different chemical elements and compounds he cannot be the omnipotent creator and sustainer of all that exists or the highest authority in the universe or multiverse.

The Axioms of Ethics

Ethics is the branch of philosophy that investigates the principles and rules to which human behaviour must conform in order to be deemed good and right. It will be argued in a next chapter that these principles and rules also amount to axioms. It will be shown that right and just behaviour is characterised by the virtues of responsibility and integrity. It will also be demonstrated that good behaviour conforms to the principles of forgiveness or tolerance and compassion or empathy.

Article 1 of the Belgic Confession, quoted previously, describes God as "completely wise, just, and good, and the overflowing source of all good". In Q & A 11 of the Heidelberg Catechism, God is described as merciful and just. These "definitions" of God contain internal inconsistencies or contradictions and, therefore, simply cannot be true.

If God is called perfectly wise, good, merciful and just, then it is implied that he conforms to certain objective or independent standards of wisdom, goodness, mercy and justice. There must, therefore, be such objective and independent standards, otherwise the notions of wisdom, goodness, mercy and justice would be without any meaningful content. These notions are, though, intelligible to all intelligent people and all will agree that these are desirable attributes or virtues.

Therefore, if God is called completely wise, good, merciful and just, then the standards of wisdom, goodness, mercy and justice have an absolute authority and he is judged to be conforming to them – be it in a perfect manner.

That means that he cannot be the supreme being and highest authority in the universe, since he does not possess more authority than these standards or rules. He has no choice but to accept and conform to these standards and rules, as well as apply them in his dealing with intelligent creatures, should he exist and desire to be perfectly good, wise, merciful, and just. This line of thought was already proposed by Plato, the ancient Greek philosopher.

Plato

Plato argued that should it happen that the gods define what is "good", then it is arbitrary and this word is, therefore, actually meaningless. If the gods are, though, inherently good, then goodness is defined independently of the gods. The same applies to the Christian God. He cannot be the author of moral standards since it is inconceivable that he could, for instance, have declared that rape and murder are commendable and good actions.[97]

One of the most well-known South African theologians of the twentieth century, the late Professor Johan Heyns, would not have agreed. He wrote in his manual on theological ethics:

> "The ethical or ethical norms cannot, therefore, be applied to God. He is supra-moral since He exists above the creation. Although he is good and acts in a good fashion, He isn't morally good and his actions are not moral actions. His goodness is divine goodness and his actions are divinely good actions. He who applies ethics, which is seated in the relationship between man and man, to God is making a creature of God – and that may not happen, just as the ethical may not be deified."[98]

This way of thinking is, unfortunately, not in line with traditional reformed thinking, as formulated in the passages from the Heidelberg Catechism and Belgian Confession, quoted above. If these creeds declare that God is good, wise, just and merciful, then these words

---

[97] Stenger, *The New Atheism,* 150; Grayling, *The God Argument,* 105.
[98] Heyns, *Teologiese Etiek,* 14–15 (own translation).

must have the same meaning when also applied to human beings – otherwise these words would be meaningless. It is simply impossible to distinguish "divine goodness" from human goodness, although it must be granted that "divine goodness" must be perfect goodness, whereas human goodness is always relative or imperfect goodness. But "goodness" is "goodness" – whether it is applied to God or to man. The same applies to God's alleged justice, mercy and wisdom. Heyns also states that moral standards are part of the created world, which means that God formulated them when he created his creation. But the question remains: did he have any choice in the matter? The answer must be "No".

If the universal ethical attributes or virtues of integrity, responsibility, compassion and forgiveness/tole-rance are axioms, they do not only apply to intelligent creatures in the created universe. Axioms are unprovable, yet eternal truths or principles and if they are eternal, then they must also apply to God – should he exist, because he won't be able to escape their validity. Should he, though, decide to act contrary to these principles, he cannot be the good, just and merciful God he is supposed to be.

Ergo: There is no possibility that a supposedly good, merciful, just and wise God can be the highest moral authority in the universe since he will be subject to the eternal and universal moral axioms or standards of goodness, mercy, justice and wisdom. Therefore, if he isn't the highest moral authority he jus cannot exist.

God's Unjust Judgments
The Bible and the Reformed creeds declare that God is absolutely just. But is that really the case?
One repeatedly reads in the Bible of Judgment Day when God will judge the godless sinners and condemn them to eternal punishment in hell. Their sins amount to a rejection of God's authority,

disobedience to his laws and an insult to his majesty. The Westminster Confession teaches in Chapter VI/vi:

> "Every sin, both original and actual, being a transgression of the righteous law of God, and contrary thereunto, doth, in its own nature, bring guilt upon the sinner, whereby he is bound over to the wrath of God, and curse of the law, and so made subject to death, with all miseries spiritual, temporal, and eternal."

On Judgment Day, God will be the aggrieved party who seeks justice against those who wronged him, insulted him, transgressed his righteous laws and commit-ted lese-majesty against him. He will, though, also be the judge on Judgment Day.

It is an axiom of jurisprudence that nobody can be a judge in his own case (Latin: *nemo iudex in sua causa*) and that a presiding officer in a hearing must be impartial. On Judgment Day, God will violate this basic rule by being judge and a party to the proceedings simultaneously.

Ergo: Since God is the aggrieved party in the case against each sinner on Judgment Day, we cannot rely on God also to be an impartial and just judge on that day. It is, therefore, impossible that a just God exists.

Impossibility to Control Cosmic Events
The Heidelberg Catechism and the Belgic Confession echo the Bible in declaring that God controls every single event on earth, including fortune and misfortune. For that to be true, is must also mean that God is supposed to be in control of everything throughout the whole universe. This earth, which we inhabit, is not an isolated spot in the huge expanse of space – it is part of everything and is influenced by

everything. The natural laws that operate on earth are the same laws that apply everywhere else in the wide universe.[99]

The question now arises: is a supposedly omnipotent and omniscient supreme being – in other words, God – really able to control all and everything in the universe? Do we see any signs of this control where the laws of nature are being suspended or violated to reach some or other mysterious goal in his creation or to avert some or other undesirable outcome? The answer must be a definite and final "No".[100]

The universe is immensely huge. With our strongest astronomical instruments we can only detect objects something like 13 billion light years away from us in any direction. Anything that is further than that is invisible and undetectable because the combined speed with which we and those objects are moving apart is greater than the speed of light. Light waves and other radiation from those extremely distant objects – if they do exist – cannot, therefore, ever reach us and we can never receive any information about them. This "bubble" with a radius of 13 billion light years around us must encompass most of the whole universe, since the universe is estimated to be $\pm 13{,}7$ billion years old.

Within this expanse of the observable universe there are between 300 and 500 billion galaxies. A galaxy can contain as much as 400 billion stars. That means that the total number of stars in the universe may very well be $\pm 1.2 \times 10^{23}$ – or just over 100 sextillion. Every one of all these stars exerts some sort of influence on the rest of the universe, however minute. Is God really controlling the movements of all these stars? Does he control how they influence each other? Is he able to know what is happening in each of these uncountable number of stars? Is he sitting at a celestial switchboard or

---

[99] Clark, *The Big Questions*, 178–79.
[100] Clark, *The Big Questions*, 162–69, 190–91; Stenger, *The New Atheism*, 83.

control board where the movements of every star is being monitored and managed? Most stars seem to be surrounded by planetary systems. Is God also in control of all these myriads of planets?

An average star weighs about 10^{35} grams. Thus, the total mass of all the ordinary matter in the universe would be about 10^{58} grams – that is $\pm 10^{48}$ metric tons. Each gram of matter is estimated to have about 10^{24} protons, or about the same number of hydrogen atoms, since each hydrogen atom has only one proton. That means that the total number of hydrogen atoms in the universe would be roughly 10^{72}. That is 10, followed by 72 zeros or something like one-hundred thousand quadrillion vigintillion.[101]

Can the God of the Bible count so far? A human being can concentrate his attention on only one thing at a time, although he can fluctuate his attention between different things. Can God – if he exists – concentrate on $\pm 10^{72}$ atoms, all at the same time and continuously?

Is God able to keep tabs on each and every atom in the universe? That must be a totally impossible task, even for a supreme being who is supposed to be omniscient, omnipresent and omnipotent. To do that, he must be aware of the position and movement of every single atom, as well as of their subatomic particles, all at the same time – together with the way they influence each other.

The problem is, though, that subatomic particles, atoms and molecules do not posses individuality – and that must be the way God designed the universe; that is, if he is the designer and creator of all. All electrons and protons look and behave in exactly the same way. All hydrogen atoms also look and behave exactly in the same way. That is also true of atoms of all the other chemical elements. Therefore, there is absolutely *no* possibility that anyone can keep track of any single individual atom – not even God. How is that to be achieved with the $\pm 10^{72}$ atoms in the universe? If God really is the designer and creator of the universe, then he must have designed and

---

[101] Villanueva, "How Many Atoms?"; Clark, *The Big Questions*, 17, 26.

created it in such a manner that it is impossible for him to control every subatomic event. If it isn't possible to know the positions and movements of all the atoms and particles in the universe and to direct them, then there is no possibility that a supreme being can be omniscient and omnipotent and be the ruler and manager of his whole creation.

Apart from that, it is an established fact in quantum physics that it isn't possible to determine both the position and speed of a subatomic particle at the same time.[102] The radioactive decay of an atomic nucleus is, likewise, essentially unpredictable. One can only calculate what the statistical probability is that a particular nucleus will decay in a given period of time. Davies assures us: "This uncertainty is not simply a result of our ignorance of all the little forces and influences that try to make the nucleus decay; it is inherent in nature itself, a basic part of quantum reality."[103] If God really is the creator and designer, then that is the way he must have made everything.

Therefore, not even God can predict what the speed or position of a subatomic particle will be at a given moment or when a particular atomic nucleus will disintegrate. Neither is he able to control these absolutely and totally random events throughout the universe, since that is the way he must have designed and created the matter of the universe – should he be the creator. The universe abounds with subatomic events with cosmic consequences. For instance, the heat from our sun is the result of nuclear reactions deep under the surface of the sun where the nuclei of hydrogen atoms are being squeezed together and merged to convert them into helium nuclei, which reactions release copious amounts of energy.[104] Since these reactions occur purely at random it is not even possible for God to predict or

---

[102] Hawking, *The Grand Design,* 86.
[103] Davies, "What Happened before the Big Bang", 32–33.
[104] Clark, *The Big Questions,* 41–42.

regulate them. Real omniscience and omnipotence are, therefore, just not attributes one can ever ascribe to a hypothetical supreme being.

Richard Dawkins mentions that the theologian Swinburne declared that a single God, who controls all the electrons in the universe, must be a simple explanation of everything happening in the universe. Dawkins finds that this cannot be a simple explanation. If God has to keep a gazillion fingers on all the gazillions of electrons in the universe and simultaneously has to react to the prayers of intelligent beings in billions of galaxies, then that cannot be a simple explanation but must be an extremely complex one.[105] One has to add: a totally impossible one – even for the Jewish, Christian, and Muslim God on account of the way the universe operates.

Stenger takes this argument further by retorting that believers may declare that God purposely made the universe in such a way that he built unpredictability on a quantum scale into his creation. That, however, means that God must have relinquished his control over creation and that all events happen without his intervention or oversight. If events happen this way and the universe runs all on its own, then we may ask: is God in any way necessary? Does he really manage our affairs and listen to our prayers as Jews, Christians and Muslims believe?[106]

We may, furthermore, ask: did God have any choice in creating the universe in any other way? Could he have constructed a universe that is not made of protons, elec-trons, neutrons and other subatomic particles? Could he have devised a universe where other forces are at work? We cannot really say, because we are only familiar with the present universe in which we live. But we can also imagine that God did not really have a choice in the matter. He simply had to abide by the fact that matter is made up of molecules, atoms and sub-atomic

---

[105] Dawkins, *The God Delusion,* 149, 154.

[106] Stenger, *The New Atheism,* 83.

particles. That means that he cannot be the supreme authority and the ultimate cause for the existence of the universe.

During recent years the concept of a multiverse has taken hold in the world of astronomy and physics. The multiverse is conceptualized as a vast collection of universes, outside our own universe, of which scientists believe that they have enough evidence to suspect or even confirm its existence.[107] That begs the question: Is a putative creator of everything in any way able to control every subatomic event and every nuclear reaction in all the stars in this vast array of universes, the multiverse? The answer cannot but be a definite "No".

Ergo: It is impossible for a God to be an omnipotent and omniscient ruler of the universe since the universe on a subatomic level does not allow him to know of and control every event on that level and, therefore, it is not possible for him to exist.

Impossibility to Break the Laws of Nature

Scientists have managed to discover a large number of laws of nature, which they express by means of mathematical formulae. The question arises: is God – if he exists – able to do anything that violates these laws? After all, he is supposed to be omnipotent and be able to do anything. A naïve or fundamentalist believer might conceivably answer that God must be able to violate these laws since he is the omnipotent author of those laws.

One can put a further question to this believer: Is God able to move a rock at a speed greater than the speed of light ($\pm$300 000 km per second)? This believer will be inclined to answer 'Yes'. It can, however, be said with confidence that God cannot do that because the speed of light is an absolute speed limit. Nobody has, in any case,

---

[107] Hawking and Mlodinow, *The Grand Design*, 18–19, 174–75, 209–10; Siegel, "This is why the Multiverse Must Exist".

observed any object in the universe moving at a speed higher than the speed of light.[108]

The reason for this is that it will take an infinite amount of energy for any object to achieve the speed of light because any object at that speed will have an infinite mass. In other words: there is not enough energy in the universe to speed up any material object to the speed of light.[109]

Ergo: If God is indeed the creator of the universe, then he designed it in such a way and formulated the laws of physics in such a manner that there is a limit to what he is able to do. He is unable, for instance, to move any object at a speed faster than the speed of light or change the laws of physics. That means that he cannot be omnipotent and, therefore, cannot exist.

Impossibility to Manage Human Affairs
The Bible also teaches us that God manages the affairs of humans and that we may pray to him to bring some or other desired result about, such as healing a sick person, averting a looming disaster or causing somebody to act in a certain way. It will be shown that this is just not possible.

The actions of humans are controlled by their central nervous systems, of which their brains are the main components. When a human brain is being stimulated mechanically, by means of electromagnetic fields, by radio-activity in the blood system or by cosmic rays, then old memories pop into consciousness or new insights appear spontaneously.[110]

---

[108] Mills, *Atheist Universe,* 154–55.
[109] Joubert, *Die Groot Gedagte,* 128–31; Clark, *The Big Questions,* 152–55.
[110] Kolb and Wishaw, *Fundamentals of Human Neuropsychology* 144–46, 286–88; Zimmer, 2003: 415; Stenger, *The New Atheism,* 180, 196; Friedlander, "Cosmic Ray".

Recent research by neuroscientists at the University of York found that transcranial magnetic stimulation (TMS) can have an influence on peoples' religious beliefs and prejudices. TMS is described as "a safe way of temporarily shutting down specific regions of the brain. The researchers targeted the posterior medial frontal cortex, a part of the brain located near the surface and roughly a few inches up from the forehead that is associated with detecting problems and triggering responses that address them." The report added: "The findings reveal that people in whom the targeted brain region was temporarily shut down reported 32.8% less belief in God, angels, or heaven."[111]

A good example of a well-known person whose thoughts and actions were possibly influenced by electro-magnetic fields, was the reformer Martin Luther. He got caught in a violent thunderstorm in 1505 and that caused him to become a monk and enter a convent.[112] It is reasonable to wonder how the electrical fields produced by the thunderstorm might have had an impact upon his brain and his subsequent decision.

Cosmic rays are high-powered particles, moving at extremely high velocities, mostly consisting of naked protons and electrons, but sometimes also of more complex atomic nuclei. They seem to be produced in far-away supernova explosions, in our sun and in other stars. We on earth are, for the most part, shielded from their damaging effects by the earth's atmosphere and magnetic field. Some of them, though, do manage to penetrate these shields. Others cause secondary cosmic particles to be created when they crash into our atmosphere, such as X-rays and gamma rays, which may also reach the surface of

---

[111] Medical Brief, 20.10.2015.
[112] Hillerbrand, "Luther, Martin".

our planet – where they might interact with the brains of human beings or cause mutations in the DNA of living beings.[113]

These cosmic rays are, therefore, sometimes partly responsible for human thoughts and actions. The behaviour and decisions of a human being is, furthermore, dependent upon a large number of other factors, such as state of health, nutrition, the actions of other people, value system, beliefs, emotional state, weather and climate, past experiences, motivation, habits, needs and abilities. The behaviour of any human being is, therefore, essentially unpredictable. The actions of cosmic particles are totally random and the other factors impacting upon a person's actions are so complex that nobody – certainly not even God – is able to predict with certainty how any person will act, feel, and think under certain circumstances.

Likewise, the radio-active decay of particles in a human being's blood and which may activate certain neurons and networks in the brain is a totally random and unpredictable process.[114]

Is God able to guide the totally random movements of a certain cosmic ray so as to influence the brain of a specific human being? Is a supreme intelligent being able to guide all the other factors, which have an impact on the choices people make and the actions they undertake? Since the movements of cosmic rays and the decay of radio-active particles are totally random and unpredictable – because that is the way God must have organised his creation, if he does exist – God just is not able to control their influence on the brains of people, or any other intelligent beings on other planets, should they exist. There is, therefore, no possibility that a highest being can control or influence the affairs of humans.

Cunningham reasons that if God is really in control of everything in the universe, including human affairs, then there is no

---

[113] Burton, "Radiation"; Friedlander, "Cosmic Ray", Rousseau, *Die Groot Avontuur,* 216.
[114] Stenger, *The New Atheism,* 196.

place for human free will. If that be the case, humans must be mere puppets in the hands of God without any volition of their own and they cannot be held responsible for their deeds or failures.[115]

Ergo: it is impossible that God exists since the universe on a subatomic scale does not allow him to be omniscient and omnipotent and to be able to control and regulate the actions, thoughts and decisions of human beings.

Omniscience and Omnipotence Incompatible
Richard Dawkins formulated the following argument to demon-strate that God's purported omniscience and omnipotence are mutually incompatible:

> "If God is omniscient, he must already know how he is going to intervene to change the course of history using his omnipotence. But that means he can't change his mind about his intervention, which means he is not omnipotent."[116]

Ergo: God cannot be both omniscient and omnipotent and therefore he cannot exist.

God's Memory
The God we encounter in the Bible is a God with a personality and a consciousness. He communicates with human beings and he has a memory because he reminded the people of Israel through his prophets, time and again, of all he has done for them in the past. In Matt 25: 34–40 we read that the heavenly judge will remind those, who are allowed to enter heavenly bliss, that they are the people who fed him, clothed him, quenched his thirst, visited him when he was sick and gave him lodging when they did these things to other human

---

[115] Cunningham, *Decoding the Language of God*, 231.
[116] Dawkins, *The God Delusion*, 78.

beings in need. A memory presupposes time since memories are records of past events. The implication is that a God, who remembers and has a memory, must also exist in time – not outside of time.

The Bible stresses the idea that time has had a beginning (Gen 1: 1; John 1: 1). This is also what the science of cosmology has found; time was created together with the universe about 13,7 billion years ago.[117] But if God exists in time because he has a memory of events in the past, he cannot have created time, he cannot be eternal and he cannot be the creator of the universe.

According to the Bible, God also has knowledge of future events. He communicated this knowledge to prophets who wrote them down as warnings or promises to his people. A number of these prophecies were never fulfilled. It seems, therefore, that God's knowledge of the future is also not perfect.

Ergo: it is impossible that an eternal God with a memory and foreknowledge can exist.

The Unknown God
A good example of those theologians and philosophers who assert that it is impossible to say anything meaningful about God is the Dutch philosopher J L Springer. He devoted a thick book of more than 300 pages to discuss thinkers in the past who wrote about God. He then came to the following conclusions:

- The existence of God cannot be proven by human reason;
- God cannot be an object of human knowledge;
- We have to acknowledge our ignorance about God and it is not even possible to assert that the word "existence" may be applied to him; and

---

[117] Hawking and Mlodinow, *The Grand Design,* 171–72, 230.

- We can only experience God existentially.[118]

This book amounts to a careful analysis, but it won't satisfy believers, as well as sceptics. Even if we depart from the traditional view about holy scripture, namely that they were directly inspired by God, and exchange it for the more liberal view that the scriptures merely contain the records of how people experienced God in the past, then the views of Springer cannot be accepted.

Even if it is so that we can only experience God existentially, then it must be possible that those experiences can and must be put into words and definite statements about God. That is what happened with the authors of holy scriptures; they left us detailed descriptions of their experiences with their God.

Springer's point of view may be characterised as the pinacle of agnosticism.

Conclusion

It has been shown that the arguments posed by believers in an endeavour to prove the existence of God, do not hold water. The God we encounter in the scriptures is not always the benevolent, forgiving, loving, just and caring deity we are supposed to worship and love. The Bible also shows a cruel, unjust, vindictive and jealous side of this supposed supreme being. Is any rational and sane human being prepared to love and worship this type of God?

Furthermore: a number of arguments have been presented to prove that it just is not possible for the God of Jews, Christians and Muslims to exist. Should he exist, he cannot be omnipotent and omniscient because he is powerless to alter the axioms of mathematics, ethics, jurisprudence and logics or to change the laws that govern the behaviour and properties of chemical elements and

---

[118] Springer, *Waar, Wat en Wie is God?*

compounds. Neither is he able to control subatomic events or the activities and processes inside the brains of human beings.

In other words – there is definite proof: this God cannot exist and, therefore, never existed. He is dead, totally dead, non-existent, gone, merely a product of people's imaginations or wishful thinking. Should somebody ask, "Who is God?", the only possible answer is: "Nobody. God isn't a 'who', a being with personality. There is no such a person or being."

The idea that there is a supernatural and spiritual, omnipotent, omniscient, omnipresent and caring creator of the universe must be classified as a widely-held fantasy, illusion, superstition or even deception – in the same category as Father Christmas, the Easter Bunny, the Abominable Snowman and the Loch Ness Monster. People of the 21st century don't believe in the ancient Babylonian, Egyptian, Greek and Roman gods anymore; more and more people are also relinquishing a belief in the deity of the ancient Israelites.

This prompts the question: if religion is built upon a fallacy and amounts to a mere superstition, namely the irrational belief that a supreme being called God does exist, then what are we to believe in its stead? Is there anything we can be certain about? The next part of this book will deal with these questions.

PART C
RECONSTRUCTION

CHAPTER 11
THE SCIENTIFIC METHOD

Introductory Remarks

The previous part demonstrated that one cannot ask: "who is God?" It is not possible to provide an answer to that question. God is not a 'who', a person, an entity or being with personality and intelligence. It is, however, meaningful to ask: "where and what is God?" This part will try to provide an answer to this question.

It goes without saying that such an answer must be rational and may not clash with established scientific insights. The concept "God" needs, therefore, to be reconstructed and stripped of its mythological, astrological and superstitious elements.

The point of departure of the philosophy presented here is the fact that there are a number of axioms on which one may build a whole body of philosophy. The most basic axiom, I propose, is the following: the universe is constructed rationally. The universe in which we live is amenable to methodical investigations and rational deductions may be made regarding its origin, composition, processes and future. This proposition cannot be proved but nobody in his/her right mind will reject it and practitioners of the natural sciences will agree with it since all the mathematical formulae that govern events and processes in the universe fit neatly and elegantly into each other.

All our explanations of phenomena in the universe, if they are to be accurate, reliable and useful, must of necessity be rational and logical. In other words: irrational or illogical explanations don't make sense, cannot be accurate and cannot be accepted. To be rational also means that all the scientific theories used to explain natural phenomena cannot contain contradictions or clash with other established theories.

Several of these axioms have already been mentioned in a previous chapter. Apart from that, it is the endeavor of this book to (re)construct a rational philosophy about God or the divine that accords with the insights of the various sciences and scientific disciplines.

This philosophy differs from post-modernism that declares that there can be no certainties and that each person has his own perspective on the world, which constitutes truth for him/her. The axioms, which are the points of departure of this philosophy, do provide certainty.

In the same manner, contemporary science also provides certainty since the technology and procedures supported by scientific findings do work without any hitches.

In the pages that follow, the following topics will receive attention:

- The scientific method as the only method to gain rational, dependable, consistent and reliable knowledge.
- The nature of axioms and the nature of reality.
- The fundamentals of ethics.
- The divine.
- The human spirit, soul and body.

What is Science?
This book purports to be scientific in nature, to take the rational scientific method seriously and to take scientific discoveries and insights into account. It is, therefore, necessary to gain greater clarity on the question: what is science? This question will be dealt with rather extensively, since many theists regard science with a certain measure of scepticism or even suspicion and distaste.

During the ages, the Church and many Christians proved to be enemies of science. The great library of Alexandria, containing more or less all the books written up to that date, was torched by Christians in 391 AD who thereby committed perhaps the most serious and horrible crime in the history of science. During the fifth century, the Church closed the schools of philosophy in Athens – the universities of those times. No empirical work was undertaken during the Middle Ages and the erroneous scientific views of Aristotle and Ptolemy were regarded as the ultimate truth, on the same level as God's revelations in holy scripture. A freethinker such as Giordano Bruno was burnt at the stake in 1600 and Galileo Galilei was forbidden by the church in 1616 to teach that the earth rotates around the sun.[119]

There are many churches and Christians who are unwilling to accept that the theory of evolution is the only rational explanation for the diversity of life forms on earth, simply because this theory is at odds with their under-standing of a text of many centuries ago, namely the first chapter of the book of Genesis.

It is not uncommon for atheists, agnostics, rationalists or naturalists to hear that they are guilty of "scientism" – a way of thinking that is supposed to be convinced that only science can produce reliable knowledge and neglects knowledge about supernatural truths. Boudry counters this attack by pointing out that there is absolutely no dependable evidence for the existence of supernatural entities and that theologians have utterly and spectacularly failed to prove with rational and scientific arguments that God does exist.[120] Barbara Smith points out that science has its limits – it cannot claim to make pronouncements regarding ultimate truths; that is the task of philosophy and theology. Scientism occurrs when scientists don't honour these limits of science. However, this does not mean that scientific insights are worthless because much

---

[119] Grayling, *The God Argument,* 107.
[120] Boudry, "The Sin of Scientism", 6.1.

valuable and verifiable knowledge has been uncovered by scientists.[121]

So, what is science? The late eminent South African Christian philosopher, Herman Stoker (1899–1993), explained correctly and accurately – in spite of being a Christian – that scientific knowledge is not simply a description of phenomena. It is systemised knowledge that endeavours to understand, to explain and to evaluate. It seeks relationships in order to combine knowledge into a system or a finished whole.[122] Heyns and Jonker, two theologians, agreed: "Science is systemised knowledge and verified knowledge of reality."[123] Maarten Boudry defined science as "encompassing all legitimate domains of inquiry based on reason and evidence."[124]

Scientific knowledge, therefore, is systematic and tested knowledge; knowledge that may be verified (or hasn't been falsified) by other investigators and observers; knowledge that tries to provide a rational or logical explanation for certain phenomena, and that makes certain predictions possible. Scientific knowledge is the exact opposite and negation of superstition, a belief not supported by solid evidence or rational deductions from established facts and accepted theories.

Science and Philosophy

The above-mentioned descriptions and definitions of science are metatheoretical or philosophical pronounce-ments. They form part of the philosophy of science. It is, therefore, necessary to investigate what philosophy is and what its relationship with science is.

---

[121] Smith, "Scientism".

[122] Stoker, *Beginseks en Metodes in die Wetenskap*, 135–36.

[123] Heyns and Jonker, *Op Weg met die Teologie*, 28 (own translation).

[124] Boudry, "The Sin of Scientism", 6.1.

Strauss calls philosophy "the science of sciences". He adds that philosophy is the science that is directed towards a coherent vision of the totality of the varieties of reality.[125]

According to Botha, there are three levels of knowledge: mundane or practical knowledge, scientific knowledge and metatheoretical knowledge. Enquiry at the metatheoretical or philosophical level endeavors to answer questions regarding the basis of the individual sciences, as well as questions regarding the theoretical substructure, suppositions and points of departure of the different scientific disciplines. Philosophy is, therefore, knowledge and insights regarding the phenomenon of knowledge.[126] It is, as it were, "the story behind the story".

It is clear on account of these descriptions that no scientist can operate without a philosophical basis. As soon as he/she reflects about the meaning and place of his subject – and that is continuously necessary – he/she ventures into the field of philosophy. Philosophy tries to gain a total vision and understanding of the cosmos; it is a synthesis of and a construction of meaning for all the different scientific disciplines. It provides answers to the questions for which the separate sciences with their investigative methods cannot provide answers.

For the philosopher, the theories and findings of the different sciences are the raw material with which he/she works. This material is assembled into a great building project in which every bit of raw material plays a meaningful role within the whole – where on its own it would perhaps be less meaningful. One can compare this process with a high-rise building. Every room in this building represents a separate science or discipline. All the rooms are being kept together by a greater framework or skeleton to form a whole, namely the

---

[125] Strauss, *Inleiding tot die Kosmologie*, 5, 7.
[126] Botha, *Metateoretiese Perspektiewe*, 8.

building itself. Philosophy provides this framework for the individual sciences.

Paradigms and Suppositions

There is a popular notion that scientists expose the truth regarding various issues by means of their experiments, observations and investigations, and that the knowledge derived thereby provides certainty or security. However, it is not quite as simple as that.

No scientist approaches his field of study in a totally objective fashion. He/she engages a myriad of suppositions and prejudices, and these influence his/she method of collecting, selecting and interpreting his data. Kitty Ferguson gives an extensive description of the factors that may influence scientific findings. The method of observa-tion, the type of instruments and apparatus utilised, the investigator's theoretical and philosophical points of departure, biases against the findings of other scientists, cultural conditioning, religious and philosophical prefe-rences, political and economic interests, and the spirit of the times all play a role in determining the outcome of a specific investigation.[127]

Many of these factors boil down to a certain philosophical inclination in the investigator. The philoso-phical postulates from which scientists take their point of departure may easily take the form of some ideology or another. Every separate science is thus characterised by a number of schools of thought or theoretical approaches, depending on the type of underlying philosophy. In Psychology, for instance, we find the psychoanalytical school of Freud with its determinism, behaviorism with its positivism, existentialism, phenomenology, the client-centered approach with its humanism, and the system theory with its holism.[128]

---

[127] Ferguson, *The Fire in the Equations*, 39-40.
[128] Botha, *Metateoretiese Perspektiewe*, 27.

One of the most influential figures in the philosophy of science during the twentieth century was Thomas S Kuhn, who introduced the concept of a scientific paradigm. He described paradigms as follows: "These I take to be universally recognized scientific achievements that for a time provide model problems and solutions to a community of practitioners."[129]

A paradigm is the intellectual framework within which normal science, the system current in a particular time period, is practised. It is a coherent tradition according to which research in a specific science is conducted. It prescribes certain points of view, standards, conventions and methods, which are accepted as axiomatic by the scientific community.[130]

He writes elsewhere that a paradigm consists of "interpretative models" and "explanatory models, models for understanding".[131] It is a constellation of convictions, values and techniques that are shared by the members of a certain scientific community. The description of a paradigm is usually found in scientific textbooks – not in research papers. The individual researchers regard it as a given and assume that their colleagues accept the same paradigm – and that facilitates communication between them.[132]

In the field of the natural sciences, one usually finds only a single paradigm, or one overarching paradigm, for each scientific discipline. However, Kuhn regards it as an open question as to whether the social sciences can be united by such paradigms.[133] It is certainly not the case in psychology; it has already been mentioned that there are a number of schools of thought active in this scientific field, each with its own philosophical assumptions. It does seem, though, that

---

[129] Kuhn, *The Structure of Scientific Revolutions,* viii.
[130] Kuhn, *The Structure of Scientific Revolutions,* 10, 11.
[131] Kuhn, *The Structure of Scientific Revolutions,* 7.
[132] Kuhn, *The Structure of Scientific Revolutions,* 19–20.
[133] Kuhn, *The Structure of Scientific Revolutions,* 15.

psychology is moving in a direction where neuroscience will be able to explain all psychological functions and problems, with the result that psychologists will in the end, perhaps, adopt a single paradigm.

That which Kuhn calls a paradigm is referred to by various other names by other practitioners of the philosophy of science. Mesarovic calls it a "general theory",[134] Küng calls it a "macro model"[135], Pieterse refers to a "metatheory" or a "basic theory"[136] and Mouton and Marais make use of the term "philosophical framework".[137]

Kuhn also introduced the concept of a scientific revolution to the philosophy of science. Such a revolution takes place when a certain paradigm becomes outdated and is no longer in a position to accommodate and explain new developments and research findings. That necessitates the search for a new paradigm. This type of revolution usually takes place gradually, since those in the scientific community who do not want to accept the new paradigm must first retire or die before their places can be taken by adherents of the new paradigm. Such a revolution seems to outsiders like a normal progression of the particular science, but for the people involved the whole world appears to have changed, as they look at it with new eyes and interpret known facts in a new way.[138]

Examples of scientific revolutions, where one paradigm displaced another, are the successive acceptance of the Ptolemaic, Copernican, Newtonian and Einsteinian world views by astronomers and physicists.[139]

---

[134] Mesarovic, "Foundations for a General Systems Theory", 4.
[135] Küng, "Paradigm Change in Theology", 9–10.
[136] Pieterse, *Praktiese Teologie*, 51.
[137] Mouton and Marais, *Basiese Begrippe*, 147–51.
[138] Kuhn, *The Structure of Scientific Revolutions*, 12, 18, 77, 92, 93, 111.
[139] Küng, "Paradigm Change in Theology", 9–10.

From this exposition it is clear that a close relationship exists between philosophy and science. They are dependent on one another. The data for the construction of a philosophical world view are provided by the separate sciences. The practitioners of the individual sciences approach their subjects with various conscious and unconscious philosophical suppositions and assumptions; the findings of science are, therefore, dependent on a certain philosophical approach.

The progress of philosophy and the separate sciences amounts to an ongoing interaction between a paradigm and empirical investigations, which consist of observations, experiments and measurements. It is a wearisome process that hangs partially in the air, because philosophy and science are interdependent. The results of science are, therefore, always tentative and always prone to revision.[140] Similarly, philosophy has not yet spoken the last word. For this reason, science is not yet a unified discipline, although that is an ideal towards which scientists are working.[141]

On the other hand, it does not mean that scientific findings are nothing but fantasies. The Nobel Prize winner, Steven Weinberg wrote: "Everything in my experience as a scientist convinces me that... one view or another bears an unmistakable mark of objective success. It certainly feels to me that we are discovering something real in physics ..."[142]

Scientific Theories

No science amounts to a mere collection of seperate facts. The separate facts are glued together into a theory or model in order to provide an oversight of the field of investigation. Theories endeavour to explain certain phenomena, seek causes and motives and express

---

[140] Ferguson, *The Fire in the Equations*, 36–37.
[141] Van Peursen, *De Opbouw van de Wetenschap*, 21–22.
[142] Weinberg, *Dreams of a Final Theory*, 149.

certain regularities in a logical and systematic way. In the physical sciences, especially physics and astronomy, such scientific laws and theories are expressed by means of mathematical formulae.[143]

A theory is nothing but a scientific endeavour to describe, explain or interpret reality or an aspect of reality.[144]

A theory is, therefore, more than simply a guess – it provides a rational explanation for observed facts and seeks connections between phenomena. A theory allows predic-tions to be made regarding the behaviour of a certain aspect of reality and the results of future investigations can be tentatively predicted. A well-known example of a scientific theory is Darwin's theory of evolution by means of which he tried to explain the large variety of life forms on earth.

Opponents of the theory of evolution often argue that the concept of evolution is "only a theory". This argument displays their ignorance. Theories are to be distinguished from guess work or hypotheses, as explained. A scientific theory is a rational and successful explanation of observed phenomena that is accepted by the majority of practitioners in that particular scientific field. In contrast, so-called "Intelligent Design", the intellectual construct of fundamentalist Christians who oppose the theory of evolution, cannot even be called a theory because it doesn't explain anything and neither can it be deemed to be intelligent or rational.[145]

Theories are usually constructed by utilising existing scientific knowledge. If new and contradictory evidence emerges, the theory has to be adapted.[146] Since theories are always tentative and prone to

---

[143] De Wet et al., *Navorsingsmetodes,* 20; Mouton and Marais, *Basiese Begrippe,* 145; Schilling, "The Threefold Nature", 82.

[144] Botha, *Metateoretiese Perspektiewe,* 25.

[145] Hitchens, *God is not Great,* 85–87.

[146] Ferguson, *The Fire in the Equations,* 41.

revision, scientists avoid speaking of the truth of a certain theory. They prefer calling theories successful or useful.

A successful theory has to fulfill certain demands:

- It must connect logically or rationally with other theories;
- It must provide the simplest explanation for certain phenomena – the so-called razor of Ockham[147];
- It must be testable; every investigator using the same methods must be able to make the same observations and deduce the same theory from these observations[148];
- That which is being explained must be clearly defined;
- It must be a logical and valid deduction from the data;
- It must provide a definitive explanation for the facts without creating new problems;
- It must be logically consistent and communicable;[149]
- It must allow for deductions and predictions – which also have to be testable;[150] and
- It must be adaptable in the light of new data.[151]

All this means that a successful scientific theory must be a rational and logical intellectual system. Flew wrote that scientists are "moved by profound reverence for the rationality manifest in existence... the grandeur of reason incarnate in existence."[152] In other words: the axioms of logics must always apply when scientists report on their findings and formulate theories.

In science one often encounters the idea of a construct. This term is used for a phenomenon that cannot be observed directly, the

---

[147] Ferguson, *The Fire in the Equations,* 41–43.
[148] Seiffert, "Einführung in die Wissenschaftstheorie", 188.
[149] Sztompka, *System and Function,* 16–23.
[150] De Wet et al., *Navorsingsmetodes,* 20.
[151] Einstein, *Mein Weltbild,* 128.
[152] Flew, *There is a God,* 102.

existence of which is inferred on account of its influence on other aspects of reality. Examples of such constructs are phenomena such as atoms, gravity, electricity, inflation, personality, intelligence or mental health. When constructing theories it is often necessary to employ such theoretical constructs as principles of explanation.[153]

The Methods of Science

It is the goal of any empirical scientific program to reach a theory that can explain all observed phenomena in a given segment of reality. There are certain steps to be followed in this process:

- *Conjecture*: certain predictions are made and suspicions are raised on account of preliminary knowledge of the subject matter and certain existing theories.
- *Expectation*: A hypothesis is formulated.
- *Testing*: An empirical investigation is undertaken to test the hypothesis and to formulate a theory.[154] A hypothesis renders a preliminary explanation for certain observed phenomena. It provides direction to the investigation by anticipating certain results. The hypothesis must be formulated in such a manner that it may be tested empirically; it must, in other words, be able to be falsified or confirmed.[155] A hypothesis that has been confirmed may be regarded as a law of nature. Both may have the same contents; a law of nature is nothing but a hypothesis that has been tested and confirmed.[156] A hypothesis or a law of nature is a generalisation from discrete phenomena.
- *Verification and falsification*: The testing of a hypothesis is always done by means of empirical methods – in other words,

---

[153] Seiffert, *Einführung in die Wissenschaftstheorie*, 190–91.

[154] Chadwick et al., *Social Science Research,* 14; Heyns and Pieterse, *Eerste Treë in die Praktiese Teologie,* 77–78.

[155] De Wet et al., *Navorsingsmetodes,* 76–78.

[156] Seiffert, *Einführung in die Wissenschaftstheorie,* 144–45.

through sensory perception, measurements and observation. The following stages may be distinguished:

- *The empirical stage*: raw data or information is collected by means of observation, measurement or experimenta-tion. The data are evaluated analytically and meticulously described. Observation means that as much information as possible regarding a certain process or state of affairs must be collected. Experimentation means that some or other process is being manipulated in order to ascertain the influence of one or more variables thereon.
- *The theoretical stage*: the observation or experiment is evaluated in order to find possible regularities. These regularities may be expressed in terms of mathematical formulae or statistics. A theory is formulated by means of induction and generalization in order to explain the observed data or regularities. In the social, cultural and behavioural sciences where human beings are being studied, it is also important to try to understand.
- *The transformative stage*: the new theory is applied in practice.

A scientist oscillates continuously between these stages. He/she can start at any of these stages and move on to the other stages, since no one has logical priority above the others.[157]

Scientific Papers

The results of scientific investigations are routinely published in learned journals. These investigations mostly take the form of experiments, observations and measurements. Some investiga-tions boil down to a meta-analysis in which the results of any number of

---

[157] Schilling, "The Threefold Nature of Science and Religion" 80–85; König, "Teologie", 23–27; Pieterse, *Praktiese Teologie,* 31–33.

related investigations are analysed and summarised to result in a more comprehensive view of a certain field of study.

Papers presented to learned journals by scientists are always scrutinised by referees who have the task to adjudicate whether the methods described in these papers are acceptable and rational and whether the results and conclusions are warranted. This process is called "peer review" and no paper in a journal can be regarded as a contribution to science if it has not been analysed and reviewed by other practitioners of that particular field of investigation.

This process is meant to ensure that published papers are of a high quality and that the contents are credible and rationally defensible.

Classification of Sciences

It is necessary to classify the various sciences in a systematic manner in order to group similar sciences together. The most popular classification is found at universities where every subject is allocated to a certain department and where departments are clustered together in faculties. This classification cannot always be justified scientifically and it is often done simply for administrative reasons.

An ontological classification principle may be used; subjects are classified according to the segment of the world or reality to which they belong:

- Physical sciences:
- Biological sciences;
- Social – or behavioural sciences; and
- Cultural sciences.

It is furthermore possible to classify sciences as either theoretical or applied sciences. In addition, there are the metatheoretical sciences such as Philosophy, Logic, Mathematics and Information Science.

A Last Thought

This exposition about what "science" entails was meant to convey the insight that science, in whatever form, leads to useful and valid knowledge.

The overriding object of all educational systems is to impart and distribute knowledge. Schools, colleges and universities all have the task to teach pupils and students and to help them to gain knowledge about the world. Universities also have the task of generating new know-ledge by means of research done by staff members and post-graduate students. The knowledge thus gained is disseminated by means of learned theses, articles in journals, and textbooks. The public media – television, radio, the internet, newspapers and magazines – all play a part in popularizing scientific knowledge.

In general, members of the public appreciate the findings of scientists. They are grateful for new and better medications, new inventions in the field of chemistry, electronics and mechanics, methods to increase food production, and explanations of how things work, *etcetera*.

Scientists – of whatever field – are trained rigor-ously in scientific methods of doing research, of investigating a certain portion or aspect of reality and how to make sense of a vast amount of information. Life in our times would not have been possible without the contributions of generations of scientists. It is, therefore, necessary to take the findings and theories of scientists seriously.

All scientists strive to obey the principle of rationality and to present their findings and theories in as rational a manner aspossible. It has to be asked at this stage: what is "rational"? It seems to be one of those basic concepts that defies accurate defining, connectd to the fundamental axion that reason can be deemed to be reasoable or rational.

A dictionary provides this definition for the word "rational": "relating to, based on, or agreeable to reason; reasonable." This is a tautology because synonyms are used to define a certain concept. Perhaps one may describe rationality as the requirement to take the rules and axioms of logic into consideration and to base all conclusions on solid evidence.

Because the universe or reality is structured rationally it is amenable to scientific investigation and description. The information hidden or embedded in all phenomena, processes, and events must, therefore, be rational in nature.

CHAPTER 12

AXIOMS

The Nature of Axioms

It has already been shown in a previous chapter that axioms are eternal and universally valid truths that cannot be proved, but are accepted as true and valid by all informed people. It has also been argued that God, regarded by theists as the highest authority in or above the universe, cannot, in fact, be the highest authority, since he is powerless to alter or amend the axioms of mathematics, logics, jurisprudence, ethics and human rights – and if he isn't the highest authority, it goes without saying that it is also impossible for him to have ever existed.

The reason why axioms cannot be proved is related to the fact that they mostly deal with the most fundamental aspects of the universe – aspects which cannot be accurately defined, such as reality, time, space, matter, energy, consciousness and informa-tion.

We often use the word *reality* without thinking about the exact meaning of this word. We often use this word as a synonym for "the world" or "the universe". The Reader's Digest Word Power Dictionary describes *reality* as something "actually exis-ting, not imaginary, not idealized or fictitious".[158]

This is not very illuminating, because it merely tells us that reality, that which exists or subsists, is not an illusion or a hallucination, but something real. This definition is nothing but a tautology – a description using other words to say the same thing. We may, therefore, declare: it is an axiom that the world or reality is real. That the world or reality is really real – and not an illusion or a

---

[158] Reader's Digest Word Power Dictionary, "Reality".

hallucination – cannot be proved but it is something that all sane people accept.

It has to be added that no two people experience reality, the world or the universe, in exactly the same way. Each one has his or her own unique perspective upon the world. But when people are communicating they are talking about the same world or reality and that makes communication possible.

It may, furthermore, be accepted as an axiom that the universe exists in *time* and *space*.

Stuart Clark states: "Time is an immensely difficult concept to define" – although all of us are aware of the passage of time "by the changing nature of events". He, therefore, does not even venture a definition of *time*.[159]

The Encyclopedia Britannica defines *time* in the following terms: "a measured or measurable period, a continuum that lacks spatial dimensions."[160] Albert Einstein defined *time* as that which can be measured by a clock.[161] These definitions are also tautologies. If one should try to define the concepts "period" and "clock", it can only be done in terms of the concept "time".

Polkinghorne, who wrote on "the nature of time", admits: "The nature of time is indeed a challenging issue." He also nowhere provides a definition of *time* and can only agree with St Augustine who famously wrote:

> "For what is time? Who can readily and briefly explain this? Who can even in thought comprehend it, so as to utter a word about it? But what in discourse do we mention more familiarly and knowingly, than time? And, we understand, when we speak of it; we understand also, when we hear it spoken of by

---

[159] Clark, *The Big Questions,* 159.
[160] Encyclopedia Britannica, "Time".
[161] Einstein, "Space-Time".

another. What then is time? If no one asks me, I know: if I wish to explain it to one that asketh, I know not."[162]

There are those who declare that *time* is an illusion, due to the fact that no two observers experience *time* in the same way.[163] It is indeed true that no two observers will ever experience the passage of *time* in the same manner. The subjective experience of *time* is different for all people. A solitary prisoner in a cell will experience *time* to be running very slowly and he will be extremely bored. A very busy person, on the other hand, feels that *time* flies.

The objective experience of *time*, as measured by a clock, may also differ, depending upon the speed with which the observer is moving. It is a consequence of Einstein's theory of special relativity that *time* slows down, as measured by a clock, when the observer and his time piece are travelling faster and faster, approaching the speed of light.[164]

That *time* is not an illusion but a part of reality is proved by the fact that the speed of light is always $\pm 300\,000$ kilometres per second – irrespective of the speed with which the light source or the observer are moving. The amplitude of the light waves may change when the light source or the observer are moving, but the speed of the light waves always stays the same.[165] Speed is always a product of *space* (he distance travelled) and *time* (the duration of the movement over the relevant distance).

Although the *experience* of *time* may be relative, that does not take away the fact that *time* is something real. After all, the universe and *time* had a beginning, $\pm 13{,}7$ billion years ago and, therefore, the

---

[162] St Augustine, *Confessions,* Book XI; Polkinghorne, "The Nature of Time", 278, 283.
[163] Joubert, *Die Groot Gedagte,* 269–74.
[164] Clark, *The Big Questions,* 154–55, 159.
[165] Clark, *The Big Questions,* 23–24, 78, 152–56.

universe is getting older as *time* goes on and its age may be calculated by observing its present state. When astronomers are observing objects further and further away from their vantage point on earth they are also looking more and more into the past since the light of distant galaxies need *time* to travel to their telescopes and other instruments. For instance, the nearest giant galaxy to our own Milky Way Galaxy, the Andromeda Galaxy (M31), is situated about 2,5 million light years away. That means that astronomers see this galaxy as it looked 2,5 million years ago – not as it is at the present because the light of its stars needed so much *time* to reach us.

Sensitive instruments in orbit around the earth have detected the afterglow of the initial explosion that caused our universe to burst into existence and expand. The extreme age of this radiation can be measured on account of its so-called redshift, the fact that the amplitude of light waves increase as the light source and the observer are moving faster and faster apart, which causes that radiation to move more and more to the red side of the spectrum.[166]

It may, therefore, be accepted as an axiom that our Universe exists in *time* and, therefore, is in a continuous state of change since its creation about 13,7 billion years ago.

The Encyclopedia Britannica provides this definition of *space*: Space is a "boundless, three-dimensional extent in which objects and events occur and have relative position and direction." This is just another circular description, since *space* is defined in terms of "extent", "position" and "direction". These terms, on the other hand, cannot be defined unless the concept "space" is used.

A dictionary defines *space* as "the three-dimensional area occupied by a material object" and "a continuous expanse".[167] These definitions are also tautologies since they use the concepts "three

---

[166] Clark, *The Big Questions*, 23–35.
[167] Reader's Digest, 1075.

dimensional", "area" and "expanse", which are merely synonyms for the word "space".

Space and *time* are irrevocably intertwined since both were created at the moment of creation, ±13,7 billion years ago.[168] Space-time may be called the "hypothetical fabric of the Universe".[169] *Space* and *time* are connected due to the fact that time slows down for any object that increases its speed. In other words – the faster that object travels in *space* in a given *time*, the slower its *time* will pass.

The example of twins of whom one is an astronaut is often used to explain this phenomenon. If the astronaut twin started a space journey to a destination far away from earth at a speed approaching the speed of light, he may measure a year for the *time* that he was gone before he returns to earth. His twin brother, who did not travel so fast and so far, will experience the *time* that his brother was gone as decades and he may even be dead when his astronaut brother returns – merely a year older in terms of his own *time* frame.

Although satisfactory definitions of *time* and *space* cannot be given, we all know very well what the words "time" and "space" mean and we use them regularly.

It may, nevertheless, be accepted as an axiom that our Universe contains *space* and exists in *space* – just as it exists in *time*. *Time* and *space* are, therefore, fundamental concepts that cannot be explained adequately but they always have to be taken into account when the Universe is to be investigated and understood.

It is not possible to provide a definition of *matter* either, since it is such a fundamental concept. The Encyclopedia Britannica ventures this definition: *matter* is a "material substance that constitutes the observable universe and, together with energy, forms the basis of all objective phenomena."[170] A dictionary tells us that

---

[168] Hawking and Mlodinow, *The Grand Design*, 127, 171–73.
[169] Clark, *The Big Questions*, 203.
[170] Encyclopedia Britannica, "Matter".

matter is "a physical substance".[171] To declare that *matter* is a material or physical substance explains nothing and it is just stating the obvious, namely that *matter* consists of *matter*.

Yet, everybody knows what we are talking about when the word "matter" is used. Victor Stenger gave this (rather unscientific) definition of *matter*: "It's stuff that kicks back when you kick it."[172]

The famous equation of Eintein, $E=mc^2$, shows that *matter* and energy are essentially the same and one may be converted into the other. In this equation, E is a symbol for energy, m is a symbol for the mass of matter and c denotes the speed of light. This boils down to the fact that a tremendous amount of energy is locked away in a tiny bit of *matter*.[173]

It may regarded as, yet, another axiom: the Universe contains matter, which may be converted into energy.

Energy may be described as "the capacity for doing work." There are various forms of energy, namely potential energy (stored in a spring or a coil), kinetic energy (movement), thermal energy (heat), electrical energy (generated my magnetism), chemical energy (when fuels are burned or chemical reactions occur) and nuclear energy (when fission takes place).[174]

Energy is expended to produce *work. Work* can be decribed as a "measure of energy transfer".[175] This demonstrates that the concept of *energy* is yet another fundamental concept that cannot be defined accurately and which can only be illuminated by using a tautology. This is no surprise since *energy* and *matter* can be converted into each other.

---

[171] Reader's Digest, 657.
[172] Stenger, *The New Atheism*, 162.
[173] Zee, *Einstein's Universe*, 164.
[174] Encyclopaedia Britannica, "Energy".
[175] Encyclopaedia Britannica, "Work".

The concept of *information* may also be regarded as such a fundamental concept. Attempts to define this concept all fail, since they also amount to tautologies and circular descriptions. The Encyclopedia Britannica, for instance, provides this description: "The term information refers to facts and opinions provided and received during the course of daily life."[176] It has to be noted that this is another circular definition, since *information* is defined in terms of synonyms, such as "facts" and "opinions". A dictionary defines *information* simply by giving the following synonyms: "knowledge, facts or news"[177] – which doesn't explain anything regarding the nature of *information*.

We all know, though, what is meant when the word *information* is used.

Information may be subdivided into the following categories:

- Descriptive and explanatory information (indicative mode);
- Commands and instructions (imperative mode);
- Wishes and speculation (optative and subjunctive modes); and
- Meta-information (the rules of grammar and logics)

To unmask or discover the *information* embedded in an object, event or process, a recorder is necessary. This recorder is usually a biological entity, such as a human being or an animal, who unlocks and gathers the information through its senses that are connected to its central nervous system. In our technological age, mechani-cal or electronic recorders, such as cameras and sound recorders, may also be used to record *information*, but this *information* can only become meaningful if interpreted by a subjective entity, such as a human being. For *information* to be useful, it has to have meaning. Raw data on their own do not convey meaning and have to be interpreted or

---

[176] Encyclopaedia Britannica, "Information".

[177] Reader's Digest, 545.

manipulated in some or other manner – by means of graphs or statistics, for instance – before it can be regarded as useful and meaningful.

When *information* is passed on from one person or entity to another person or entity, communication occurs. *Information* between people can be passed on by means of symbols, comprised of words (spoken or written – in any human language), mathematical formulae, gestures, facial expressions, tone of voice, touch, music, and pictures. *Information* between machines is passed on by means of mechanical indications or by means of electronic impulses. Animals and humans also communicate with each other through odors.

It is possible to provide inaccurate, unclear, incom-plete or untrue *information*. But it will always be possible to unmask untruth when it clashes with the axioms or rules of logics and when the axiom that every assertion must be backed up by evidence, is disregarded.

Another fundamental concept that defies definition is *consciousness*. Ratey informs us: "Attention and consciousness are inexorably intertwined, and some scientists now believe that they are actually the same thing. Despite the volumes that have been written on conscious-ness, we still don't know how to define it, or what brain activity gives rise to it."[178]

Kolb and Wishaw declare: "Conscious experience is pro-bably the most familiar mental process that we know, yet its workings remain mysterious. Everyone has a vague idea of what is meant by being conscious, but consciousness is easier to identify that to define." They nevertheless venture this definition: "[T]he level of responsiveness of the mind to impressions made by the senses …."[179] This definition also tells us nothing – it uses the concept "mind", which is simply a synonym for *consciousness*. Russel reminds us: "This is the paradox of consciousness. Its existence is undeniable, yet

---

[178] Ratey, *A User's Guide to the Brain,* 111.
[179] Kolb and Wishaw, *Fundamentals,* 645.

it remains totally inexplicable." The only definition he can provide is to call it "inner experience"[180] – which isn't very illuminating.

Horgan finds: "A theory of consciousness would represent the apogee – the culmination – of neuroscience."[181]

It may, nevertheless, be regarded as an axiom that normal human beings have *consciousness* when they are not asleep or in a coma and that they are aware of the fact that they are conscious. The seat of *consciousness* or awareness inside the brain has not yet been discovered and there are those who think that it will never be precisely located since it may depend upon the interplay between various parts of the brain.[182] The concept of (self)-consciousness will receive more attention later in another chapter.

Axioms as the Foundations of Science
It may be, furthermore, regarded as an axiom that science would not have been possible without investigators and observers who possess (self-)consciousness. These scien-tists collect informa-tion, which they use for the creation of rational theories to explain certain aspects of reality.

Science cannot operate without axioms. The discipline of logic, which uncovers the formal structure of valid arguments and methods to verify or falsify knowledge or information, rests upon a number of unprovable axioms. All sciences endeavour to uncover valid and useful knowledge. If the information thus presented and the theories formulated thereupon display logical incon-sistencies or other logical flaws, then it is clear that that information and those theories are false and useless.[183]

---

[180] Russel, *From Science to God,* 27, 32.
[181] Horgan, *The End of Science,* 161.
[182] Encyclopedia Britannica, "Consciousness"; Papineau and Selina, *Introducing Consciousness*.
[183] Schagrin, "Logic".

It is common knowledge that the rules of logic are applied on a daily basis in courts of law; if the evidence given by a witness violates the rules of logics, then that evidence cannot be true. The object of cross-questioning in a court case is always to try to poke holes in the testimony of a witness and to uncover inconsistencies by the application of the axioms or rules of logics.

There is no overarching axiom of logics from which all the other axioms may be deduced. There is a multiplicity of logical axioms or theorems, but they all conform to the fundamental rational principle that they tie in neatly with each other and that they do not contradict each other.

The discipline of mathematics, which uncovers and describes the formal structure of reality, likewise, rests upon a number of unprovable axioms. Sciences and disciplines such as physics, engineering and astronomy cannot operate without mathematical formulae, which are the embodiment of their theories. It may be said that mathematics is the language of natural science. Biological sciences and social sciences cannot progress without mathematical statistics.[184] Chemistry depends on the fact that the properties and behaviour of elements and compounds demonstrate that they are ruled by immutable laws.

All these axioms and the systems built upon these disciplines have a prescriptive or regulative function. Logic prescribes how true and reliable knowledge must be structured. Natural laws, formulated by means of mathematical formulae, describe how the universe or reality is structured. Antony Flew wrote: "The important point is not merely that there are regularities in nature, but that these regularities are mathematically precise, universal, and 'tied together'."[185]

The practice of science, therefore, demands the minds of rational and (self-)conscious investigators who can gather and store

---

[184] Berggren et al., "Mathematics"; Lambek, "Mathematics".
[185] Flew, *There is a God*, 96.

information and knowledge in their own memories, by mechanical means on paper and electronically and who can also formulate rational and logical scientific theories.

All these mathematical axioms – mathematicians have not yet found all of them and there may be an almost infinite number of these axioms – also conform to the rational principle that they support each other and do not contradict each other.

Naturalism and Rationalism
The philosophy subscribed to by most scientists may be called naturalism, apart from the fact that it may also be characterised as rationalism. This philosophy may be described by means of the following propositions, which may be regarded as axiomatic:

- Nature is all that exists; there is simply no evidence of supernatural entities;
- The universe or reality is made up of only four basic or fundamental things or ingredients that cannot be properly defined or described – as has been demonstrated above – namely space, time, matter/energy and information;
- Biological organisms with sense organs and consciousness are needed to uncover and gather the information embedded in the world to convert that into knowledge by recognizing something as food, as dangerous or harmful, as useful, as annoying, *etcetera*;
- Nature organises itself according to fixed rules or laws of nature and is not governed or influenced by spiritual or supernatural forces;
- The universe as such has no overall purpose or meaning that can be discovered, although individual human beings can lead meaningful lives;

- Science has always been able to explain and understand nature through observation, measure-ment and experimentation without invoking super-natural explanations;
- Everything has a cause; events don't just happen, there are always causes or reasons for the occur-rence of an event or the existence of a certain state of affairs and these causes or reasons can be discovered by utilising appropriate investigative methods;
- The attributes and actions of all living beings, including humans with their ability to talk, think and plan for the future, are the result of evolution;
- Religious faith and superstitions have caused much misery and evil in the world; and
- Morality exists independently of the God of conventional religion and people are able to adhere to moral rules without any religious faith.[186]

It may also be seen as the most basic axiom in science that all descriptions and explanations of the world must be rational and obey the rules of logic. When I was a student, I happened to read an article by the Dutch philosopher, Arnold Loen. He posed the question: Is reason reasonable? He came to the conclusion that the rationality or reasonableness of the human faculty of reasoning cannot be proved because it would amount to a circular reasoning. I would like to add: it is not necessary to prove that reason is reasonable, since it may be regarded as a self-evident truth or axiom that the human faculties of reason and reasoning are reasonable or rational. One may confidently state that the principle of rationality is the most basic principle in science.

---

[186] Stenger, *The New Atheism,* 160; Graffin and Olson, *Anarchy Evolution,* 6, 213.

For instance: in his book, The Selfish Gene (1976), biologist Richard Dawkins demonstrated convincingly that evolution by means of natural selection is a very logical or rational process. When taking into consideration all the environmental factors that organisms have had to contend with during the history of the earth, it becomes clear that biological evolution is an inevitable process.

Scientific Axioms
All the empirical sciences are built upon the following rational suppositions or assumptions, which may be also seen as axioms:

- *All phenomena in the world are amenable or open to scientific investigation.*

Up to date, scientific investigations have unraveled a large number of the mysteries of the universe. Using appropriate methods and instruments, scientists were able to uncover the information and knowledge embedded in any conceivable phenomenon, event or process in the universe. This information amounts to a description of the qualities of the particular phenomenon, event or process, as well as an explanation why this state of affairs is the way it is and it is recorded by means of words and sentences in any human language, as well as mathematical formulae, graphs, statistics and pictures. We still don't have a so-called "theory of everything" to explain how the four fundamental forces of nature may, perhaps, be unified. We still don't have an explanation for the origin of life on earth, although there are some educated guesses. There is still much to be discovered about the functioning of the human brain, but we already do have a large body of knowledge in this regard. We cannot explain the phenomenon of consciousness yet [although it may be predicted that we will never be able to do that and this position is explained later on]. But, scientists are confident that their investigations will eventually be able to unravel all or almost all of the mysteries of the universe. John Horgan already predicted more than two decades ago in 1998 that the end of science is upon us. That means that most of the mysteries of the universe have been clarified and very little of fundamental nature remains to be discovered.[187]

- *Scientists are able to gain accurate and useful knowledge about the world.*

The sophisticated technology and procedures we have in our time is proof of the fact that theoretical scientists have uncovered knowledge about the world that may be regarded as valid, reliable and useful and that this knowledge was applied successfully to develop technological marvels in the fields of engineering, chemistry, medicine, agriculture, *etcetera*.

- *There are no supernatural phenomena and the universe or reality consists of only the following fun-damental elements that cannot be defined adequately: space, time, matter/energy, informa-tion, and consciousness.*

Scientists have been unable, up to date, to find any sign of a supernatural reality. Every investigated phenomenon can, in principle, be reduced to physical and chemical processes – even thought processes and emotional upheavals inside a human being's brain, as well as psychological disorders. Information is immaterial in nature, but it needs a material substrate to be stored. Information is also embedded in all phenomena, processes and events in the world and, there-fore, it is possible to give relevant and adequate descriptions and explanations of these phenomena, processes and events, thereby uncovering the information embedded in these phenomena, processes and events. Knowledge can be described as an accurate rendering or description of the information embedded in phenomena, processes and events. Of course, it won't be possible to unearth all the information about anything, since every description and explanation can always go into greater detail.

---

[187] Horgan, *The End of Science,* passim.

- *Every assertion or scientific theory must have sufficient proof for it to be accepted.*

This axiom is also one of the axioms of jurisprudence. Sufficient proof for a theory means that other investigators must be able to replicate the initial investigation and verify or confirm its results. Victor Stenger wrote: "Faith is belief in the absence of supportive evidence. Science is belief in the presence of supportive evidence."[188]

One may add: only the application of rigorous scientific methods can lead to reliable knowledge, consisting of facts and theories. Quoting from an ancient religious text tells us next to nothing about how the world works or what the nature of reality is. These texts only have historical value – they tell us how certain people in the past viewed the world to make sense of events in their lives.

---

[188] Stenger, *The New Atheism*, 15.

CHAPTER 13

FUNDAMENTALS OF ETHICS

Religion and ethics

Ethics is another branch of philosophy that rests upon a number of axioms and it is necessary to discover and explain these axioms.

Singer defines ethics as "the discipline concerned with what is morally good and bad, right and wrong,"[189] Although the concepts "good" and "right" overlap to a certain extent, they are not identical. The same applies to their antitheses, namely "bad" and "wrong".

The concepts of *goodness* and *rightness* are basic or fundamental concepts, which cannot be defined – just as concepts such as *reality, space, time, matter, consciousness* and *information* can also not be defined adequately. It is only possible to give synonyms for these concepts. *Goodness* can be described as morally excellent, well behaved. For *rightness*, the following tautological defini-tion may be given: moral correctness. These descriptions or definitions, really, don't say anything. Yet, everybody knows very well what *goodness* and *rightness* mean.

Because *goodness* and *rightness* are such fundamental concepts, one can expect them to be connected to some moral axioms – as will be demonstrated later on.

Many people think that ethics and religion go hand-in-hand and that without religion there cannot be any morals. This is a fallacy. Buddhism and Confucianism are both Eastern philosophies or religions without a deity and yet they have highly developed moral or ethical systems. It can be demonstrated that the crime rate tends to be

---

[189] Singer, "Ethics".

higher in countries where the Christian religion has a foothold – especially in those countries where Protestantism is the dominant variety of Christianity. In other words: religious people are not necessarily moral people and people without religion may, in many cases, be moral examples.

The late Prof Johan Heyns did not think this way. He wrote: "The ethical does not find its foundation in itself, not in man and also not in anything that is part of the cosmic reality, but solely and only in God."[190] He also argued that knowledge of that which is moral or ethical can only be gained from God's special revelation in Holy Scripture.[191]

Although Johan Heyns commanded great respect during his lifetime, one cannot agree with his dogmatism on this point since it can be disproved by the available evidence. That there are ethical axioms, independent of religion, will be argued at length in the pages to follow.

On the other hand, Stenger showed convincingly that morality must have had an evolutionary origin. The development and acquisition of moral attributes such as altruism and cooperativeness towards one's relatives and neighbors has been proven through the ages to be advantageous for the survival of the individual and his offspring, as well as for his group.[192]

Shermer shows that the sharing of the proceeds of hunting or gathering in smaller nomadic groups was and is always fair. Everybody got an equal or fair share, even if he did not participate in the hunting expedition or gathering foray. Cheating was unthinkable because the survival of the group depended upon fair and equitable sharing and mutual trust. Cheating only became possible when mankind became urbanised and the individual could disappear into the

---

[190] Heyns, *Teologiese Etiek*, 89 (own translation).
[191] Heyns, *Teologiese Etiek*, 110–34.
[192] Stenger, *The New Atheism*, 153–55.

multitude. That was the point where morals had to be connected to religion. God or the gods were declared to be the law-givers and invisible all-seeing inspectors of people's actions in an endeavor to deter cheaters, thieves and liars from getting away with their evil deeds.[193]

Shermer also refers to international studies of identical twins who were reared separately that showed that moral instincts are largely transmitted genetically. Upbringing and education play a minor role in this respect.[194]

Graffin and Olson declare: "Empathy is the best basis for human ethics that we have. It provides a solid foundation for strong personal relationships and a productive society." [195]

Primates, including human beings, have so-called mirror neurons in their brains. These neurons enable them to imitate the actions of others and to feel the same emotions displayed by others. This is the neurological basis for empathy – the ability to imagine and understand how another person might feel under certain circumstances. Empathy with its biological basis, therefore, makes virtues such as forgiveness/tolerance and compassion possible.[196]

Schools of Moral Philosophy

There are various "schools" or approaches regarding the foundations of ethics and it is necessary to describe each of them briefly, before explaining an own approach. Alfred Allan remarked: "A vexing question in ethics is whether it is possible to have a single set of ethical principles that is universally applicable across societies

---

[193] Shermer, *The Believing Brain*, 167–68.
[194] Shermer, *The Believing Brain*, 168–69.
[195] Graffin and Olson, *Anarchy Evolution*, 185.
[196] Kolb and Whishaw, *Fundamentals*, 582.

and time."[197] Various answers have been attempted and Allan provides a useful summary of these:

- *Absolutism and Deontologism*:

Allan describes these approaches as follows: "Absolutists maintain that there are absolute moral truths that should apply to everyone because they are universal and operate across cultures and generations. Examples of norm systems that profess to be absolute and universal are the Ten Commandments and, in recent times, the Universal Declaration of Human Rights."

"Deontologists... believe that people have a duty to follow certain principles or rules, and most believe that these principles are universal and that people must apply them irrespective of the circumstances and consequences. Certain acts are therefore wrong in themselves and are prohibited, even though they may be morally admirable or morally obligatory."

There may be a single fundamental ethical principle (monism) or a number of such principles (pluralism).[198] Possible sources of deontological principles are religion, natural law, social contract, pure reason, or common morality[199]

The best known exponent of deontological theory was Immanuel Kant who taught that one could discover ethical principles through rational thought. He believed in a "categorical imperative", an unconditional moral law, which simply had to be obeyed: "Du sollst, denn Du kannst." According to Kant, the most basic moral law would be that one would wish that his own set of moral principles would be applicable to the whole of mankind.[200] That more or less boils down to the golden rule that Jesus gave us: "Therefore whatever

---

[197] Allan, *Law and Ethics in Psychology*, 18.
[198] Allan, *Law and Ethics in Psychology*, 18–20.
[199] Allan, *Law and Ethics in Psychology*, 20.
[200] Allan, *Law and Ethics*, 22; Bird, "Kant, Immanuel".

you desire for men to do to you, you shall also do to them..." (Matt 7: 12). Esterhuyse calls this approach the rule-bound approach.[201]

Reformed theology traditionally took this position. The Heidelberg Catechism declares in Q & A 3 that we can only know our sinful state by comparing ourselves with the law of God, which requires from us to love God and our neighbor. In Q & A 91 "good works" are described as those, "which proceed from a true faith, are performed according to the law of God, and to his glory; and not such as are founded on our imaginations, or the institutions of men."

However, one may ask in this regard: which objective standards should in that case apply? If nobody can pinpoint them, then the outcome is nothing but relativism.

- *Relativism*:

According to Allan, "relativists deny the existence of an absolute or objective standard by which to judge moral positions, and they maintain that right or wrong is always relative to the specific circumstances and beliefs of the person… or group of persons…."[202]

This is an untenable position for the following reason: This approach claims to be true, acceptable, and correct. That implies that at least one universal moral truth or principle is true, namely the principle that there are no absolute moral standards. This amounts to a *contradictio in terminis* and, therefore, this approach cannot be upheld.

- *The Consequential Approach:*

Esterhuyse describes this approach as pragmatic. No action in itself is morally good or bad and one has to decide whether that action is

---

[201] Esterhuyse, *Sake-Etiek in die Praktyk,* 21–25.
[202] Allan, *Law and Ethics in Psychology,* 18.

acceptable or not by taking into account the consequences of that action.[203]

- *Pluralism*:

Allan notes: "Pluralists believe that there are many different ethical perspectives on an issue, each of which contains part of the truth, and that some are better than others, but that none of them contains the whole answer. (...) However, contrary to relativists, they believe that there are objective standards."[204] This is also the position of Esterhuyse: One has to apply both approaches when making moral decisions.[205]

Natural Law and Natural Ethics

After World War II the absolutist or deontological approach with its roots in natural law has won wide acceptance. This became especially clear in key documents, such as the Universal Declaration of Human Rights, the German Constitution and the South African Constitution. Roman-Dutch law, as expounded by Grotius, Huber and Voet during the seventeenth century, has its roots in the doctrines of natural law. The Constitution of the USA with its bill of rights also rests upon the notion of natural law.

The Universal Declaration of Human Rights (1948), the Federal German Constitution (1949) and the South African Constitution (1994 and 1996) each contain provisions regarding universal human rights. Devenish affirms that the thinking of the highest court in South Africa, the Constitutional Court, is also largely based on the tenets of natural law.[206]

Hugo Grotius (1583–1645) claimed that all nations were subject to natural law and he "insisted on the validity of the natural

---

[203] Esterhuyse, *Sake-Etiek in die Praktyk*, 17–20.
[204] Allan, *Law and Ethics in Psychology*, 19.
[205] Esterhuyse, *Sake-Etiek in die Praktyk*, 25.
[206] Devenish, *Commentary*, 630–31.

law 'even if we were to suppose... that God does not exist or is not concerned with human affairs.'"[207]

The American Bill of Rights, contained in the amendments to the Constitution, guarantees the following unalienable human rights: freedom of religion and speech, the right to defend oneself by the use of arms, the right to security and privacy, the right to a fair trial and the right not to be punished in a cruel manner.

In the aftermath of the Second World War, when the horrors of the Nazi-regime in Germany were exposed, the need arose to put the notion of human rights on a more secure footing. That prompted "the desire to invoke rules of right and justice held to be natural rather than merely conventional."[208] The doctrines of natural law also rest on other notions, besides those of human rights, for instance the rules of natural justice as explained in a previous chapter).[209] These rules are applied in courts of law and may be seen as the basis of the whole system of law.[210] This certainly applies to most other sophisticated judicial systems on earth.

The preamble to the Universal Declaration of Human Rights declares a faith in "fundamental human rights, in the dignity and worth of the human person and in the equal rights of men and women", as well as the "observance of human rights and fundamental freedoms." These values are echoed in the first three articles of the German Constitution and in the Preamble and sections 1 and 7 of the 1996 South African Constitution.

The Universal Declaration of Human Rights, the German Constitution and the South African Constitution are not merely legal documents; they also contain ethical principles and values. A

---

[207] Encyclopedia Britannica, "Natural Law".
[208] Encyclopedia Britannica, "Natural Law".
[209] Devenish, *Commentary*, 466, 472.
[210] See for instance: Transman (Pty) Ltd v Dick and Another 2009 (4) SA 22 (SCA); Von Mehren, "Contract".

comparison of, for instance, the 1996 South African Constitution with the 1983 Constitution, shows that the last-mentioned document was only meant to guide the administration of the country. The preamble to the 1983 Constitution declared that it had as its aim "to safeguard the integrity and freedom of our country ... [and] to secure the maintenance of law and order..."

On the other hand, the 1996 Constitution safeguards in sections 1, 23, 33 and 35 the principles and values of human dignity, freedom, equality, fairness and natural justice, together with the principles of compassion and care for children and those in need in sections 26–29.

Devenish remarks that "jurisdictional thinking" in South Africa before the adoption of the 1994 Interim Constitution was dominated by the notion of "parliamentary sovereignty", while the new thinking is based upon ethical values, as enshrined in the 1996 Constitution. He adds that the Bill of Rights presupposes the tenets of natural law regarding human conduct and "laws should be subject to fundamental and immutable precepts which have a natural or divine origin and sanction."[211] It may be safely said on account of the preceding that the notion of natural law, as well as natural (absolutist) ethics, has won wide acceptance in law internationally. It is, therefore, possible to discover universally accepted fundamental ethical principles and values, which apply to all people – even to all intelligent, self-conscious, rational and sentient beings in other parts of the universe, should they exist. Lennick and Kiel in their book on Moral Intelligence state: "We believe that these universal principles exist, even though we know they are not universally applied." They add: "Moral viruses are unfounded negative beliefs that are in conflict with universal principles."[212] These universal and fundamental legal and ethical principles may be seen as axioms or self-evident, rational

---

[211] Devenish, *Commentary*, 3, 634.
[212] Lennick and Kiel, *Moral Intelligence,* 35, 69.

moral truths or principles. That the system of government and law must indeed rest upon the principle of *rationality* has been confirmed by the South African Constitutional Court in 2000:

> "It is a requirement of the rule of law that the exercise of public power by the Executive and other functionaries should not be arbitrary. Decisions must be *rationally* related to the purpose for which the power was given, otherwise they are in effect arbitrary and inconsistent with this requirement. It follows that in order to pass constitu-tional scrutiny the exercise of public power by the Execu-tive and other functionaries must, at least, comply with this requirement. (. . .) What the Constitution requires is that public power vested in the Executive and other function-aries be exercised in an objectively *rational* manner."[213]

Neural Networks Involved in Moral Choices

The fundamentals of morality is not only being investigated by philosophers and lawyers, but also by neuroscientists.

To behave ethically correct, a person has to be able to perform abstract logical and moral reasoning and to choose between various possible behaviours. For that, an intact and fully developed adult brain is a necessity.[214] Our drives often conflict with each other and these may clash with our need to act cooperatively and altruistically. "Making decisions between our sometimes competing drives requires

---

[213] Pharmaceutical Manufacturers Association of SA and another: In Re Ex Parte President of the Republic of South Africa and Others 2000 (2) SA 674 (CC) at 709D (emphasis added).

[214] Lennick and Kiel, *Moral Intelligence*, 64, 69; Kolb and Whishaw, *Fundamentals of Human Neuropsychology*, 635, 666.

us to make moral choices. It is our moral intelligence, the ability to balance competing drives that makes us truly human."[215]

According to Lennick and Kiel, it has been shown that people with brain injuries mostly "simply lacked the basic neurological equipment to distinguish between right and wrong" and "no amount of education could rectify this."[216] Apart from an intact brain, proper education and nurturing by parents are necessary. Nida-Rümelin and Singer noted:

> "Wir bestrafen und belohnen das Kind in der Absicht, seine Hirnarchitektur so zu prägen, dass es später Entscheidungen treffen wird, die mit den sozialen Normen der Gesellschaft, in welche es integriert werden soll, conform sind."[217]

The cortical areas of the brains of children who have not been exposed to "good enough parenting" and who experienced abuse and/or neglect are on average 20–30% smaller than those of children who have had "good enough parenting". There are fewer connections between parts of the brain and "without those connections, no empathy is realized, and without empathy, you have impaired morality."[218]

Persons with certain psychiatric disorders, such as an antisocial personality disorder (psychopathy), depression, bipolar disorder, anxiety disorders, attention-deficit/hyperactivity disorder, and autism, often have certain defects in the architecture of the brain as a result of prenatal or postnatal injury and trauma, genetic defects, diseases during infancy and exposure to noxious substances. These disorders are usually associated with frontal lobe abnormalities or

---

[215] Lennick & Kiel, *Moral Intelligence*, 32.
[216] Lennick and Kiel, *Moral Intelligence*, 64.
[217] Nida-Rümelin and Singer, *Erregungsmuster und Gute Gründe*, 268–69.
[218] Lennick and Kiel, *Moral Intelligence*, 26.

pathology.[219] People with these disorders often lack a moral compass. Likewise, it has been found that people who use cannabis regularly run the risk of damage to the frontal cortex – which impairs their (moral) decision-making ability.[220]

To behave morally, a person needs to experience regret after having done something wrong or bad. That presupposes the construct of a conscience. Brain scans have shown that the dorsolateral prefrontal cortex, parietal cortex and right orbitofrontal cortex become active when a person experiences regret.[221] (See the illustration to locate these brain structures.)

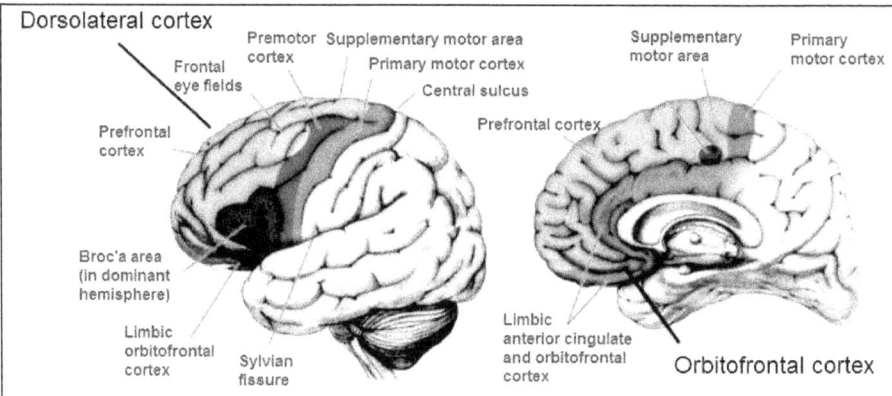

The human brain from the outside and the inside, showing the location of the dorsolateral prefrontal cortex and orbitofrontal cortex. The frontal lobe is the whole area in front of the central sulcus. The parietal cortex (not indicated) is located immediately behind the primary motor cortex and the central sulcus.[222] The cortex is the outermost layer of the brain in which the cell bodies of most neurons are located.[223]

---

[219] Aminoff, *Encyclopaedia of the neurological sciences*, 49–50, 395; Nida-Rümelin and Singer, *Erregungsmuster*, 69.
[220] Churchwell, "Altered Frontal Cortical Volume".
[221] Kolb and Whishaw, *Fundamentals*, 572.
[222] Kolb and Whishaw, *Fundamentals*, 376–77, 430.
[223] Kolb and Whishaw, *Fundamentals*, 72–73.

As with many other cerebral functions, the construct of the human conscience does not seem to be located in a single spot in the brain, but is spread out over several areas.

Morality does seem to have an evolutionary origin. Lennick and Kiel point out:

> "It is likely that altruistic and cooperative behavior is part of basic human behavior today because it was crucial to the survival of our early human ancestors. People who banded together were better able to master the elements, fight off predators, and acquire food. Individuals who cooperated and helped others tended to live longer. They were more likely to procreate and thereby get their traits into the gene pool. (…) It's not hard to see how the Golden Rule might have evolved – treat others as you would like to be treated – as a practical principle for living harmoniously and working for the common good."[224]

Stephen Pinker declares that higher animals (including humans) are capable of love and care, therefore, prepared to demonstrate altruism and care-taking of others, especially their kin.[225]

Richard Dawkins cites research that demonstrated that normal human beings have a "moral instinct" that works more or less the same in all, irrespective of religious convictions or the lack thereof.[226] This all points to the conclusion: "It's clear we are programmed to be moral."[227]

Shermer points out that a human society cannot survive without mutual trust; the members of the society must trust each

---

[224] Lennick and Kiel, *Moral Intelligence*, 31.
[225] Pinker, *How the Mind Works*, 400–01.
[226] Dawkins, *The God Delusion*, 225–26.
[227] Lennick and Kiel, *Moral Intelligence*, 30.

other not to cheat and lie if that society is not to disintegrate.[228]

Keith Ward acknowledges that atheists may have moral rules, but he argues that for them these rules are merely human inventions.[229] Johan Heyns was of the opinion that secularized man does not know love, rather has hate and positive disregard and disinterest and cold indifference, or egoistic interest and abuse, or fear and flight in his relationship with his fellow man.[230]

These points of view cannot be sustained and they do not tally with scientific findings and everyday experience. It will be argued that ethical principles are eternal axioms and that all rational and sane human beings, whether they are religious or not, acknowledge the existence of these principles.

Ethical Axioms

Fundamental and universal ethical principles display the character of axioms or self-evident eternal truths or prescriptions. These ethical axioms have a prescriptive and regulative function and describe how humans ought to behave.

The ancient Greek philosopher Plato already had the insight that there exist eternal ethical axioms – although he didn't use precisely these words. He posed the question whether the gods loved pious and holy people because they were pious and holy or because the gods loved holiness and piety as such.[231] We may translate this question into contemporary language as follows: Does God approve of the actions of good people because these actions are good, or because he approves of goodness as such? This dilemma can only have one solution: goodness, as such, exists independently of God – should he exist.

---

[228] Shermer, *The Believing Brain*, 45.
[229] Ward, *Is Religion Irrational?* 140.
[230] Heyns, *Teologiese Etiek*, 22.
[231] Shermer, *The Believing Brain*, 45.

The most basic question is: which are these ethical axioms? Lennick and Kiel found that there is more or less consensus that the following universal and fundamental moral principles exist:

- *Integrity* Acting consistently with principles, values, and beliefs
  Telling the truth
  Standing up for what is right
  Keeping promises and being dependable

- *Responsibility* Taking responsibility for personal choices
  Admitting mistakes and failures
  Embracing responsibility for serving others

- *Compassion* Actively caring about others
- *Forgiveness* Letting go of one's own mistakes
  Letting go of others' mistakes[232]

Instead of "forgiveness", one might use "tolerance", which is a somewhat broader concept.

This is an elegant scheme. Integrity and responsi-bility deal with that which is right. Compassion and forgive-ness/tolerance describe goodness. These axioms are, therefore, embodiments of the fundamental concepts of "rightness" and "goodness".

There is support for this classification from other sources. Alfred Allan investigated the ethical rules for the practice of psychology in some English-speaking countries and Europe and made lists of the ethical principles contained therein. The following is a summary of his findings:

- Responsibility (5X)
- Integrity (5X)

---

[232] Lennick and Kiel, *Moral Intelligence* 77–78.

- Non-maleficence and beneficence (1X)
- Respect for human rights and human dignity (5X)
- Competence (2X)
- Justice (1X)[233]

Integrity and responsibility enjoy wide support as universal ethical principles among psychological fraternities. Non-maleficence and beneficence may be equated with compassion, while respect for human rights and dignity, which also receives much support, may be connected to tolerance.

Stephen Pinker copied a list of "human universals" as published in 1991 by Donald E Brown on account of the investigations of ethnographers on various societies throughout the world.[234] It is possible to classify these universals dealing with morals under a number of headings.

The following human universals may be arranged under the heading of *Integrity*:

    Distinguishing right and wrong
    Law (rights and obligations)
    Redress of wrongs
    True and false distinguished
    Fairness (equity), concept of
    Moral sentiments
    Resistance to abuse of power, to dominance

The following universals may be classified under *Responsibility*:

    Murder proscribed
    Sanctions for crimes against the collectivity
    Self is responsible
    Sexual regulations

---

[233] Allan, *Law and Ethics*, 114–22.
[234] Pinker, *The Blank Slate*, 435–39.

The following may be arranged under *Compassion*:
> Cooperation
> Cooperative labour
> Empathy
> Reciprocal exchanges (of labour, goods, or services)
> Hospitality

The following universals may be classified under *Tolerance*:
> Conflict, mediation of
> Good and bad distinction

From this, it may also be deduced that *integrity, responsibility, compassion* and *tolerance* are indeed universal ethical principles and, therefore, eternal ethical axioms.

It ought to be clear that these moral principles and axioms are not derived from any religious system, although it must be admitted that holy books such as the Bible and the Qur'an do contain numerous moral prescriptions. If the above-mentioned ethical principles are truly universal and axiomatic then these holy books only reflect and repeat what already existed from all eternity as independent and universal axioms. They are also not derived from the statutory corpus of any country.

John Humphreys remarked that we do not commit all sorts of crimes due to fear for punishment, but because we know them to be wrong. "We have known that ever since we became 'civilized'."[235]

Human Rights in the South African Constitution

The Constitution of the Republic of South Africa was more or less finalised during 1996. This Constitution, with its Bill of Rights, is regarded internationally as a model constitution. It enshrines certain

---

[235] Humphreys, *In God we Doubt,* 245.

rights, which rest upon certain ethical and judicial values. Section 7 of the Constitution spells these out:

> **"7. Rights**
> 1. This Bill of Rights is a cornerstone of democracy in South Africa. It enshrines the rights of all people in our country and affirms the democratic values of human dignity, equality and freedom."

- *Human dignity* may be connected to the fundamental value of compassion, as well as the respect for the human rights of others
- *Equality* finds expression in the values of fairness and equitability
- *Freedom* cannot exist without responsibility.

It is clear, therefore, that the "democratic values" on which the South African state is supposed to be built, can be seen as an expression of the four core ethical values, together with the rules of natural justice and the axioms of human rights. All these aspects are somehow or other rationally tied together.

The Existence of Evil

Many people see life as the continuous struggle between good and evil, right and wrong. They even interpret this as warfare between God and Satan. Since moral axioms don't have the same ontological status as the axioms of mathematics and the axioms of logics, they depend on the free choices of intelligent and conscious beings to be obeyed and realized. People must make a conscious choice to behave in a certain way and, thereby, to do that which is good or that which is right. In contrast, the universe and material world operate automatically and absolutely in accordance with the the axioms of mathematics.

But people may also choose to do that which is wrong or bad. They may, therefore, promote evil. But evil does not have an independent existence, such as the axioms of morality. Evil is merely the negation or conscious denial of that which is good or right. Evil does not have an independent existence, such as that ascribed to the Devil in Christianity and Islam. The Devil may be seen as the personification of that which is bad or wrong, of evil, but that doesn't mean that evil as such is an independent force in the universe. It is totally dependent upon that which is good and right to exist and it only amounts to a conscious decision to disobey, deny or negate these moral axioms.

In other words: the existence of the moral axioms of *integrity, responsibility, compassion* and *forgiveness/tole-rance* only become apparent when conscious and intelligent beings obey the prescriptions of these axioms and reject and avoid that which is bad and wrong. These moral axioms may also be disobeyed or violated and then evil appears as the opposite or rejection of these axioms. Then dishonesty, untruthfulness, irresponsibility, cheating, selfishness, hate, cruelty, revenge, and lack of remorse become visible in the actions of these beings. Evil, therefore, is not an independent force; it is rather a parasite, a moral virus, clinging to the fundamental virtues of integrity, responsi-bility, compassion and forgiveness/tolerance, sucking the life out of these virtues.

Evil, however, is in a certain sense necessary for the existence and recognition or the fundamental ethical axioms. Goodness and rightness can only become apparent and visible when contrasted with badness and wrongness. Nobody would really understand what integrity, responsibility, compassion and forgiveness mean if there were no people who acted without integrity, responsibility, compassion and forgiveness and everybody acted automatically in an appropriate and exemplary way.

CHAPTER 14

THE MIND OF GOD

Eternal Axioms

It has become clear that there are a number of axioms, namely self-evident, eternal and universally applicable truths, laws and rules that cannot be proved but are accepted by all informed and rational people. These may be summarised as follows:

- The material world is structured in such a manner that all the regularities can be described and expressed by means of mathematical formulae; mathematics is a complex symbolic system that is built upon certain axioms;
- Information, consisting of descriptions and explanations of phenomena, given by means of mathematical formulae, in a human language or by other symbols, as well as instructions and wishes, must be rational and adhere to the rules or axioms of logics to be valid, true and useful;
- The practice of jurisprudence in the courts of the world rests upon a set of rational legal axioms, the rules of natural justice;
- The axioms on which the rights of intelligent, rational and self-conscious beings rest, are those of human dignity, equality and freedom;
- All countries, societies and groups have to be ruled, managed and organised according to fixed rules and power has to be divided into legislative, executive and jurisdictional branches; and

- To behave morally, an intelligent and self-conscious being has to adhere to the prescriptions of a number of rational ethical axioms, namely responsibility, integrity, compassion and forgiveness/tolerance.

These axioms can be divided into two categories:

- descriptive (the axioms of mathematics and logics); and
- prescriptive (all the others).[236]

The common denominator of all these axioms, the basic principles according to which the universe and a human society operates, is the principle of *rationality*.

It has been demonstrated in a previous chapter that the God of theists, of conventional religion, cannot exist, since he – should he exist – is powerless to change, amend or abolish any of these rational axioms and rules. If he is powerless then he cannot be the omnipotent supreme being presented in the scriptures as the highest authority and designer/creator of the universe. Since these axioms are eternal, immutable and universally applicable, one may declare them to be the divine principles underlying the whole of reality.

We may, therefore, accept that there are eternal principles that rule all of reality, comprised of time, space, matter/energy and information. There are intelligent and self-conscious biological entities, called human beings on the planet Earth, who are able to investigate reality and discover these eternal, rational and divine principles.

This position cannot be described as classical atheism since it recognises the existence of eternal and universal principles, laws, rules and axioms that permeate the whole of reality and may be deemed to have divine status. There is, however, no need for an intelligent,

---

[236] Benedict, *The God Debate*, 154.

omnipotent, omniscient and spiritual supreme being who thought everything out and who keeps everything going.

These eternal truths and principles were usually ascribed to the mind of God. It has been shown, though, that we do not need the mind of an omniscient, omnipresent, and omnipotent perfect supernatural supreme being to explain where these axioms and rules have had their origin. They didn't have an origin since they are timeless, eternal and universally valid. They simply exist and nobody thought them out. They are given with the existence of a material universe in which conscious and rational beings developed who are able to discover and uncover those axioms.

These sets of rational axions may, nevertheless, be described as the mind of God – but then of an impersonal entity or deity.

Other Theologians and Philosophers

There are some theologians, scientists and philosophers who have had almost similar thoughts. The Greek philosopher Plato is the first to come to mind, but attention will also be given to Ward, Davies, Armstrong, Hawking, De Klerk and Esterhuyse.

Plato drew a distinction between the physical world, which is constantly changing, and an eternal and unchanging spiritual realm of ideas or forms. These forms are the embodiment or templates of concepts such as beauty and justice. There are forms for every category of phenomena in the world, such as mankind, animal species, trees, but also of shapes, colours, beauty *per se* and justice *per se*. The highest level of the hierarchy of eternal ideas or forms is the idea of the Good, also called the One.[237] Plato regards the form or idea of the Good as a perfect, eternal, and changeless entity or idea existing outside space and time, in which all particular good things share, or "participate," insofar as they are good.[238] In other words, Plato saw

---

[237] Barnes, "Plato".
[238] Singer, "Ethics".

some "forms", which may perhaps be equated with axioms, as the underlying principles on which the world is built. He also saw an ethical principle, the Good, as the highest form and unifying idea in his eternal realm of ideas.

Keith Ward agrees with Plato that God can be equated with the idea of "the supreme Good."[239]

Paul Davies declared: "These rules [according to which the universe is structured] look as if they are the product of intelligent design. I do not see how that can be denied." If one wants to believe that they are the product of a personal creator, one may do so, but nobody can prove it. One can perhaps conceive of God "as merely a mythical personification of such creative qualities, rather than as independent agent."[240]

Karen Armstrong wrote extensively about religion and theology. Three of her most well-known books are A History of God (1994), The Battle for God (2001) and The Case for God (2009). Her concept of God, however, intentionally stays vague and nebulous. Here are some of her pronouncements to demonstrate this:

- "… inadequate images of the Absolute".[241]
- "… the transcendent reality".[242]
- "God was experienced as an imperative to action".[243]
- "The Holy Other".[244]
- "The divine".[245]

---

[239] Ward, *Is Religion Irrational?* 29.
[240] Davies, "Is there need for a divine designer?" 281.
[241] Armstrong, *A History of God*, 447.
[242] Armstrong, *A History of God*, 448.
[243] Armstrong, *A History of God*, 450.
[244] Armstrong, *A History of God*, 450.
[245] Armstrong, *A History of God*, 451; Armstrong, *Islam*, 310, 313.

- "[T]he very word 'God' is only a symbol of a reality that ineffably transcends it".[246]
- "The inaccessible, hidden source of the reality that we know as 'God'".[247]
- "[T]he utterly transcendent divinity which forever eludes us".[248]
- "Idolatry has always been one of the pitfalls of monotheism. Because its chief symbol of the divine was a personalised deity, there was an inherent danger that people would imagine 'him' as a larger, more powerful version of themselves".[249]
- "[T]he unknown and undefinable God".[250]

She does seem to equate God or "the divine" with ethical imperatives, such as the call to compassion.[251]

Stephen Hawking, the late paralyzed genius and scientist, told John Humphreys: "One could define God as the embodiment of the laws of nature."[252] This is almost the position explained in this book, although the laws of nature and the axioms underlying and ordering the whole of reality are not quite identical.

The late *Willem de Klerk*, a former professor of theology at the Potchefstroom University in South Africa and newspaper editor, wrote a book about the "strange God and his people". He declined to give a description or definition of God and declared that God is essentially

---

[246] Armstrong, *A History of God*, 455.

[247] Armstrong, *A History of God*, 460.

[248] Armstrong, *A History of God*, 461.

[249] Armstrong, *Islam*, 308.

[250] Armstrong, *Islam*, 313.

[251] Armstrong, *Islam*, 314-316.

[252] Humphreys, *In God we Doubt*, 54.

unknowable. We can only talk about him by means of analogies. He also seems to equate God with all that is good and beautiful.[253]

Willie Esterhuyse, retired professor of philosophy at the Stellenbosch University in South Africa, wrote a book about God. He says that he grew out of the naïve faith of his youth where he saw God as the ruler of the universe. He refuses to give a description of God and refers to him simply as "the divine". The divine finds its expression in principles such as righteousness, justice, compassion, care for others and responsibility.[254]

Although he does not explicitly state that these ethical principles are synonyms for God, that is, nevertheless, the implied message of his book. It appears, therefore, that Plato, Davis, Armstrong, Ward, Hawking, de Klerk and Esterhuyse more or less agree with the thesis proposed here that the axioms of morality are eternal and divine principles – apart from the idea that the divine also encompasses the axioms of mathematics, logics, human rights and jurisprudence.

Certain biblical authors also thought along similar lines:

Wisdom in Proverbs

The concept of "wisdom" plays an important part in the book of Proverbs in the Old Testament. The Hebrew word for wisdom (חָכְמָה – *chokma*) may be applied to ethical and religious insight.

In chapters 7–9 of Proverbs, wisdom is presented as a beautiful woman. The author advises his son: "Tell wisdom, 'You are my sister'" (Prov 7: 4). This woman is seen as the personification of all that is good and right, as well as the principles according to which God created the world.

In Prov 8: 22–30, Lady Wisdom declares:

---

[253] De Klerk, *Die Vreemde God en sy Mense*.
[254] Esterhuyse, *God en die Gode van Egipte*.

> "Yahweh possessed me in the beginning of his work, before his deeds of old. I was set up from everlasting, from the beginning, before the earth existed. When there were no depths, I was brought forth, when there were no springs abounding with water. Before the mountains were settled in place, before the hills, I was brought forth; when he established the heavens, I was there; when he set a circle on the surface of the deep, when he established the clouds above, when the springs of the deep became strong, when he gave to the sea its boundary, that the waters should not violate his commandment, when he marked out the foun-dations of the earth; then I was the craftsman by his side."

This all means that the author of this book – according to tradition, it was King Solomon – saw wisdom, knowledge, insight, and the laws of nature as eternal, as almost something divine.

The woman Wisdom proclaims furthermore:

> "I hate pride, arrogance, the evil way, and the perverse mouth. Counsel and sound knowledge are mine. I have understanding and power. By me kings reign, and princes decree justice. By me princes rule; nobles, and all the righteous rulers of the earth" (Prov 8: 13–16).

Lady Wisdom also states: "I walk in the way of righteous-ness, in the midst of the paths of justice" (Prov 8: 20).

In other words: Lady Wisdom personifies and encompasses such abstract ethical notions as justice, fairness, righteousness, honesty, humility and truthfulness. Wisdom, as a set of personified ethical principles, has an own, almost independent, existence.

The Gospel and Epistles of John

The author(s) of the Gospel of John and the Epistles of John seem(s) to have had a philosophical inclination and God is often equated with certain abstract principles – rather much in the same way as was argued above. It is not impossible that John was influenced by the philosophy of Plato and other Greek philosophers.

The first sentence in John's Gospel reads as follows –

> "In the beginning was the Word, and the Word was with God, and the Word was God."

The key word in this verse is λόγος (*logos*). It is usually translated as "word", but it has a rich meaning and history. Apart from "word", it may also mean speaking, speech, saying, account, reason, decree or precept. The Encyclopedia Britannica provides this background:

> The logos is "in Greek philosophy and theology, the divine reason implicit in the cosmos, ordering it and giving it form and meaning. (. . .) The idea of the logos in Greek thought harks back at least to the 6th-century-BC philosopher Heracleitus, who discerned in the cosmic process a logos analogous to the reasoning power in man. Later, the Stoics, philosophers who followed the teachings of the thinker Zeno of Citium (4th–3rd century BC), defined the logos as an active rational and spiritual principle that permeated all reality. They called the logos providence, nature, god, and the soul of the universe, which is composed of many seminal logoi that are contained in the universal logos."[255]

The Gospel of John clearly presupposes this classical Greek background when using the concept of "logos".[256]

---

[255] Encyclopedia Britannica, "Logos".
[256] Arndt and Gingrich, *A Greek-English Lexicon*, 480.

John 1: 1–5 may be seen as a summary of the creation myth of Genesis 1 where the creator is depicted as ordering everything into existence by his creative word or decree (after all, both Genesis and John's Gospel start with the same phrase: "In the beginning…"). One may, therefore, declare that – in John's view – God and the logos, the rational principles embedded in the world, are one and the same. This is almost the same as declaring that the divine is comprised of all the eternal rational axioms and rules of mathematics, logics, jurisprudence, governance, human rights. and ethics.

The first letter of John (1: 1–2) equates the "logos" with "life". God is, in addition, called the "truthful" (ἀληθής – *alethes*) in John 3: 33 and 8: 26. In 1 John 4 one reads the following statements:

- "He who doesn't love doesn't know God, for God is love" (vs 8).
- "We know and have believed the love which God has in us. God is love, and he who remains in love remains in God, and God remains in him" (vs 16).

The key phrase in both these verses is ὁ θεὸς ἀγάπη ἐστίν (*ho theos agape estin* – God is love). The word used for "love" has a broad meaning: brotherly love, charity, affection, good will, love, benevolence. In these two verses, John equates God with the idea or principle of love – which may be seen as a synonym for the basic ethical virtues or moral axioms of compassion and tolerance/forgiveness. In other words – even John had the insight that these virtues *per se* are divine and eternal.

John also wrote in 1 John 1: 5 –

> "This is the message which we have heard from him and announce to you, that God is light, and in him is no darkness at all."

Here we read: "God is light". The Greek word for "light" (φῶς – *fōs*) has many meanings: light, brightness, truth, spiritual purity, reason and mind. Here God is, in other words, equated with the abstract principles of spiritual light, purity, reason and truth. The identification of God or the deified Christ with "light" is also found in John 1: 1–5: 8: 12; 9: 5; 12: 35, 46. The "light" is contrasted with "darkness" – a metaphor for all that is bad or evil.

According to John 14:6, the following words are ascribed to the deified Jesus:

> "Jesus said to him, 'I am the way, the truth, and the life. No one comes to the Father, but by me.'"

The words "I am" (Ἐγώ εἰμι – *ego eimi*) hark back to Exod 3: 14 where God introduced himself to Moses as "I am who I am". The words "I am" are often placed in the mouth of Jesus by the Gospel of John in order to express the oneness of the deified Christ with his heavenly Father (John 6: 20, 35; 8:58; 11: 25 and 18: 5).

When the divine Jesus declares that he is "the way" (ἡ ὁδὸς – *he hodos*), he means the right way of living, following the correct ethical principles. When he also says that he is "the truth" (ἡ ἀλήθεια – *he aletheia*), he actually says that he or God and the abstract principle of "truth" or "truthfulness" are one and the same.

When he calls himself "the life" (ἡ ζωή – *he zōe*), Jesus means the abstract idea of life in its fullness, ethical and spiritual.

In John 15: 26 we read of the "Spirit of truth". The deified Jesus calls himself "the resurrection and life" in John 11: 25.

In other words: John identified God and the divine Christ repeatedly with abstract principles and ideas. He, though, also saw God as a person. He even made a deliberate grammatical error by using the third person masculine pronoun (ἐκεῖνος – *ekeinos*) when referring to the Spirit of God – instead of the more correct impersonal pronoun (it) (John 16: 8, 13). In other words: For John, therefore, God is the personification of the abstract divine principles or ideas of logos, reason, truth, love, light and life – very much as Plato thought.

And that is exactly what has been proposed above: The name "God" is nothing but a synonym for all the eternal rational axioms, laws, rules and principles that rule the universe and the realm of information. These eternal axioms and principles also provide guidance to intelligent, rational and self-conscious human beings when they endeavour to act ethically correctly.

The Noosphere

The next question that needs to be answered, is this: where are all these rational axioms, laws and principles to be found? Where do they reside? An easy answer is: in the noosphere. This is a name that may be given to the sphere or realm in which information and knowledge exist. The word "noosphere" is derived from the Greek words νοῦς (*nous* – "mind") and σφαῖρα (*sphaira* – "sphere").

The noosphere is, therefore, the realm of information, knowledge, axioms, laws. principles and rules. This term was invented by the French paleontologist, philosopher and theologian, Pierre Teilhard de Chardin, for the dimension of human thought.[257]

As has been shown, a definition of information or knowledge cannot be given, since it is such a fundamental concept – although everybody understands what is meant by this word. The noosphere may be regarded as the "space" in which all information and knowledge is situated. Information is embedded in the phenomena, processes and events of the world and has to be unearthed, uncovered, discovered and gathered through experience, observation, experimentation and rational deductions.

That leads to descriptions and explanations in one of the many human languages, but may also take the form of mathematical

---

[257] Encyclopaedia Britannica, "Teilhard de Chardin, Pierre".

formulae or statistics. Information or knowledge is not material in nature, but needs material substrates to be recorded and stored: human brains with their memories, inscriptions in clay, stone or on paper or electronic traces recorded on a computer's hard drive. Every person who is computer-literate knows the expression "cyberspace". That is the imaginary space in which websites, e-mails and other digital paraphernalia reside – although all these are actually only electronic traces on some or other computer's memory on its hard drive or an external storage device, such as a CD.

The noosphere is, likewise, the "space" in which all information and abstract rules exist – also information about information, namely meta-information, the axioms and rules that have been identified. These axioms exist independently from the physical universe and transcend it. One may even declare that the axioms of mathematics, the rules of logics, human rights, ethical principles and the rules of jurisprudence as eternal truths did not come into being when the universe exploded into being about 13,7 billion years ago, but that this meta-information in the noosphere exists outside of time and space – which gives it eternal and even divine attributes.

The eternal rules of logics, ethics, natural justice and human rights have a prescriptive function. They may be disobeyed when people are telling untruths, disregard the rights of others and trample upon basic ethical principles or virtues. But disobedience does not cause these rules to disappear; they retain their validity, even if people ignore them and act in defiance of them.

It has already been stated that the universe is comprised of four elements: space, time, matter/energy and information, as well as the consciousness of intelligent biological entities. Part of this vast body of information, namely meta-information, the eternal and universal axioms, transcend space and time and simply exist.

CHAPTER 15

THE HUMAN SPIRIT, SOUL AND BODY

Unity and Multiplicity

The relationship between a human being's physical body and his purported spirit or soul has kept philosophers busy through the ages.

It may be helpful to approach this problem from the following point of view: When two people encounter each other, they recognise each other as fellow human beings – not as objects in the world, such as furniture, machines, rocks, plants or animals, but as persons. Each one experiences the other as another "ego", another "I" or "me", which is not "I" or "me", the observer. Each one of us has the capacity of self-consciousness and we perceive that the person we encounter also has a self-consciousness, an "ego".

Peter Russel puts it aptly:

> "But what exactly is this sense of 'I-ness'? I use the word "I" hundreds of times a day without hesitation. I say that I am thinking or seeing something, that I have a feeling or desire, that I know or remember something. It is the most familiar, most intimate, most obvious aspect of myself. I know exactly what I mean by 'I' – until I try to describe it or define it. Then I run into trouble."[258]

There have been various attempts to define the concept "consciousness" or "awareness"– but without success. This concept is one of those basic concepts connected to some or other axiom. It may

---

[258] Russel, *From Science to God,* 80.

therefore be accepted as an axiom that normal and awake human beings are conscious of the world, but that they are also conscious of themselves and of the fact that they are conscious. One may also accept that animals are conscious of the world, but that they usually lack self-awareness.

Neuroscientists and psychologists make use of the concept of "theory of mind" to explain why human beings can infer that other humans have thoughts, feelings, perceptions, motives and are self-conscious. This seems to be connected to the fact that humans have mirror neurons in their brains, which enable them to have empathy with others, that is, to imagine themselves in the shoes of other people – as has been explained above.

Mirror neurons are also seen as the explanation for the fact that emotions are contagious. Even babies show this phenomenon. When one, for instance, starts to cry it will not take long for others in the vicinity to pick up that baby's distress and start crying as well. A manual of neuropsychology gives this description of the role of mirror neurons:

> "The ability of mirror neurons to have a role in self-action as well as in the perception of action of others, suggests that they provide the substrate for self-awareness, social awareness, and awareness of the intentions and actions of others and that they are likely important for gestural and verbal language."[259]

In other words: mirror neurons make self-awareness possible, although the "I", the " ego", who is aware or conscious of itself, cannot be so localised.

What is this "ego"? Where is this self-consciousness situated within the visible body? The traditional instinctive and religious view was always that a human being consists of a physical body and a

---

[259] Kolb and Whishaw, *Fundamentals*, 233.

nonphysical soul, his self-consciousness, his "ego". The soul must be spiritual in nature, it is argued, because it is invisible, ungraspable. That human beings are instinctive dualists, has already been argued.

We have also argued in chapter 4 that science has, as yet, failed to find this "soul" or "spirit" of a human being.

The proposal that I am providing here as a solution to this problem is the combined brain child of two eminent philosophers: Karl Heim (1874–1958), a German philosopher and theologian, and Victor Frankl (1905–1997), an Austrian psychiatrist and philosopher.[260]

We have this paradox: a human being, a person, is a unity – but he also seems to be a multiplicity. He seems to be more than just a body, a biological entity. He also has a psychological or nonphysical aspect – his intelligence, abilities, thoughts, feelings, values, memories and ideals, for instance. He also has this ungraspable element: self-consciousness or an "ego". How can we solve this paradox?

Paradox

The fact that a human being is a unity, but also a multiplicity, seems to be a contradiction. It is, however, only a paradox – not an insoluble contradiction. One may explain this by way of an analogy.

Think of two two-dimensional geometrical figures: a circle and a square. No-one in his right mind will confuse them. It can in no way be said that they represent the same thing:

---

[260] Heim, *Christian Faith and Natural Science*; Heim, *Glaube und Denken*; Frankl, *Das Menschenbild der Seelenheilkunde*; Frankl, *Grundriß der Existenzanalyse und Logoterapie.*

If one, however, leaves the two-dimensional level and moved to a three-dimensional level one can see the unity and identity of the two figures without any problem.

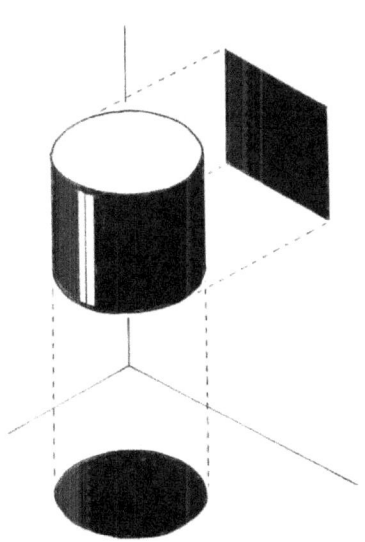

Now think of a cylindrical object, such as a tin of canned fruit, of which two shadows or projections from different angles are cast onto the wall and onto the floor with light sources to one side or from above. One shadow is square and the other is circular; the cylinder is, however, one single object.

It is possible to explain the unity and the multiplicity of a human being by using this analogy. The soul and the body can, in a certain sense, be regarded as projections of the spirit (the cylinder) on a lower level, on a lower dimension.

It is not possible to observe or experience the spirit of a human being, his "ego", with our sense organs, since it occupies a higher dimension; on the other hand, the physical/biological and psychological aspects and functions of an individual are observable.

The "Ego" not Observable

The reason that the spirit of a human being, his "ego", his self-consciousness, his mind, is not perceivable or observable, is also connected to the fact that the "ego" of an individual is in the present, while his body and soul are already fixated in the past.

This can be explained as follows: our sense organs can only observe things that are in the past. The light that strikes the eye so that it can see any object in the world needs time to travel from the observed object to the eye. Light waves always travel at a constant speed, namely $\pm 300\ 000$ km per second. In the case of stars in space, the light they radiate takes years to travel to us. Astronomers can see far-away galaxies with their telescopes of which the light took millions and even billions of years to reach us. In other words, they see these galaxies as they actually were millions or billions of years ago, not in their present state.

The light from the sun takes seven minutes to strike the earth. When we look towards the sun, therefore, we see the sun as it was seven minutes ago, not how it is in the present. Should the sun somehow miraculously disappear, we will only become aware of that fact seven minutes after it had happened. The light from an object a meter away from somebody's eye – such as the computer screen in front of me – takes a tiny fraction of a second to travel to the eye, but it is still a certain length of time. In the same way, sound takes time to reach somebody's ear from the source of the sound.

Nerve impulses from the eye and the ear have to travel a certain distance within the brain before they are registered somewhere in the brain and brought to consciousness – and that takes some additional time.

The "ego" or mind, the (self-)consciousness of a human being, cannot be observed, however, since it is the "ego" that experiences and observes the passage of time and objects situated in the past. The "ego" cannot experience itself; all that the "ego" can experience are the contents of consciousness, such as memories, thoughts and sensations.

In the same way no eye can see itself and no hand can grasp itself. The "ego" can, therefore, never be in the past in the same way as the objects in the world it perceives; it can only be in the present, the moment of "now". And that is the reason why the "ego" cannot be an object in the world, such as stars, rocks, trees, houses or animals – it cannot be objectified since it is subjective. However, the physical and psychological aspects of an individual can be observed, since they are fixated in the past. These aspects are projections of the "ego" that are fixed in the past and are, therefore, observable. It is, therefore, clear that there cannot be a separate human "soul" or "spirit" that survives death. Psychologists and neuroscientists have for decades tried to locate consciousness in the brain or to define consciousness in terms of brain activities – but to no avail.[261]

Human (self)-consciousness, the "ego", simply cannot be observed and captured since it is not fixed in the past as are all other objects that are observed or experienced. It is the subjective "agent" that experiences the world that lies in the past, while staying in the present, the moment of "now" that glides along with the passage of time as it continues relentlessly.

Human Knowledge

Human knowledge does not consist of true or accurate mental images of objects found in the world outside the human being's consciousness. How will anybody ever know whether the "images" in his mind or consciousness correspond with the objects in the "outside world", which they are supposed to represent? Humans are only aware of the contents of their consciousness or mind. On the other hand, human beings also do not have knowledge of a world constructed by

---

[261] Papineau and Selina, *Introducing Consciousness*.

themselves as is sometimes asserted – otherwise they would only know illusions and hallucinations.

A human being observes, experiences and knows the real world – but as the world appears to him. He never gets a complete picture, since he only has a certain perspective on the world. His sense organs are not only receptors but also filters that do not register certain signals. Those aspects of the world that do appear to him are also interpreted against the background of his memories, emotions, beliefs, values, expectations, goals, interests, preferences and dislikes. It is, therefore, clear that the world does not appear in the same way to any two people. However, since it is always the same world that appears to both of them, communication between them is possible.

Each person perceives himself to be the center of the world. He sees sights and hears sounds from the world from the perspective of the point in space, which he occupies. No two people can have the same perspective on the world because they cannot occupy the same vantage point at the same time.

Human knowledge consists of the contents of consciousness. In order to be true, this knowledge must correspond with the truth about the world. Truth is not, as is often said, the correspondence between knowledge and existence (reality); it can rather be described as the correspondence between the contents of a (human) consciousness or information that has been fixated by means of a code (for instance, information expressed in language or symbols and letters on paper or in a computer's memory) on the one hand, and the information embedded in events, processes or phenomena in the world.

Because it is always the "ego" that observes, interprets and knows we will never understand the nature of knowledge fully. Neuroscience has not, until now, been able to understand how memories are stored in the human brain. It is supposedly a chemical process, but the exact mechanism has yet to be discovered.[262] This "ego" is never available for observation or analysis. Similarly, human freedom will always remain a riddle since the "ego", which is free and takes certain decisions or makes plans for the future, stays hidden.

Although human freedom may be regarded as a riddle and some neuroscientists and others deny that it even exists, it is taken for granted in all legal systems of the world. It is assumed that a wrong-doer or criminal freely chose to pursue a certain course of action, that he/she is responsible for his/her deeds and he/she must face the consequences of his/her actions and misdeeds.

---

[262] Moser and Moser, "Understanding the Cortex", 67–69

CHAPTER 16
AFTERWORD

Good Work by Religious Organizations.
The contents of this book mat be disturbing to many believers because it has been shown that many of their cherished beliefs cannot be upheld any longer and that the belief systems of their churches, synagogues or mosques are nothing but antique superstitions.

It has to be granted: during the past many churches and religious organizations have done much to improve the lives of untold numbers of people by their charitable initiatives, by insisting on ethical behaviour in all walks of life and providing education. These bodies deserve the gratitude of humanity.

But that it is not to say that their dogmas, creeds, and belief systems are to be accepted without question by people of the 21st century. By now, it ought to be clear a religious faith doesn't rest on solid evidence and may to be discarded. The inevitable outcome will be that religious communities will wither, shrink and eventually die.

Type of Philosophy
The question may arise: what type of philosophy was presented in the preceding pages? Most philosophies have names, such as existentialism, idealism, empiricism, materialism *etcetera*. What name can be given to this type of philosophy?

- It cannot be called classic *atheism* since it has been demonstrated that there are eternal principles or axioms that govern the universe and ought to direct the actions of intelligent and self-conscious beings. These axioms may be regarded as divine in nature since they are timeless and

universal. Apart from that, the epithet "atheism" is misleading since it only denotes that the philosophy of theism is rejected; it does not signify what the purported atheist does believe in. Furthermore – the name "atheism" is regarded as a dirty word in Christian circles and "atheists" are pictured as the lowest form of life imaginable who may be discriminated against since they are all deemed to be amoral, immoral, and despicable personages.
- It cannot be seen to be *agnosticism* since it has been demonstrated with certainty that the God of Christians, Jews and Muslims never existed, except in the minds of believers.

By which name should the philosophy presented here be characterised? The following names may be appropriate:

- One may certainly call it *rationalism*. We may be convinced that the universe is constructed along rational lines and that the axioms of mathematics, logics, ethics, human rights, governance and jurisprudence – all of them thoroughly rational – govern the universe and ought to direct the actions, relationships and communications of intelligent self-conscious beings. The principle of rationality is, therefore, the overarching principle that encompasses the whole of reality, composed of space, time, matter/energy and information. The most basic axioms are the axiom that there are rational axioms applicable to the totality of reality, together with the axiom that reason is really reasonable or rational. It may, therefore, be characterised as a rational philosophy built upon a numbr of axioms that do not contradict each other and fit nicely together into a system of principles.
- This philosophy can also be regarded as *naturalism*. The universe is all that exists – apart, perhaps, from other possible universes of which we have absolutely no direct knowledge.

The universe is, though, governed by a number of rational mathematical, logical, ethical and juridical axioms residing in a realm of meta-information. The universe is comprised of all the matter, energy, and forces that have been discovered, as well as the information about the universe that is embedded in all the phenomena, processes and events inside the universe, together with time and space.

- It won't be wrong to call this philosophy *humanism*. We ought to feel positive about human rights, human dignity, human freedom and human equality. We should have empathy with people who are in trouble, feel miserable, are faced by their own guilt and cannot cope with life.
- Perhaps one may also describe this philosophy as *axionism*. This philosophy is convinced that the universe is being ruled by the eternal and rational axioms of mathematics, logic, ethics, human rights, governance, and jurisprudence.

The main conclusion of this book is that the principle of *rationality* is the overarching principle that encompasses the whole of reality. Human beings with their sophisticated brains and intelligence are able to reason, to think rationally. That is what they try to do when they do science or have to make important decisions. But that is not to say that human beings always act and think rationally. They mostly act instinctively and/or emotionally and even irrationally. But neuroscience has demonstrated that there are rational reasons why people do act in this manner.

John Barrow devoted a whole book, *The Artful Universe,* to point out that the make-up of the universe – all the laws of natures, the structure of mathematics and the complexities of life made possible by these laws and structures – all have a deep-seated beauty. The most wonderful aspect of all this is the fact that we humans have developed the ability through evolution to appreciate the wonder of this beauty.[263]

This book contains a joyful and positive message to believers and non-believers:

- *There is positive and conclusive proof that the God worshipped by Christians, Jews and Muslims cannot exist and just never existed, but must be declared to be a fiction or fantasy;*
- *We have no need of a supreme being whom we have to fear or worship and we can lead perfectly happy, productive, moral and meaningful lives without religion and without a temple, mosque, synagogue or church;*
- *Christianity – together with Judaism and Islam – is rooted in an ancient, outdated, prescientific, superstitious and primitive world view that cannot be maintained or updated any longer;*
- *The views found in religious scriptures regarding God, heaven and the universe cannot be reconciled with contemporary established scientific insights;*
- *The universe or reality is ruled by eternal, beautiful, universal, and rational axioms, principles, and laws, which may be regarded as having absolute (divine) authority and validity;*
- *The universe or the whole of reality is constituted of the following constituent elements or ingredients: space, time, matter/energy and information;*
- *We human beings of the species homo sapiens have sophisticated brains, which enable us to act wisely, rationally and ethically and to investigate the whole of reality and to be amazed by the wonders and beauty we are bound to find;*

---

[263] Barrow, *The Artful Universe*.

- *With our sophisticated brains, we are constantly seeking the meaning of life and of all the misfortunes that befall us and we are only satisfied with meaningful, logical and rational answers; and*
- *It is possible to ask:* Who where, and what is God? *It is clear that God is not a "who" – a being with personality. The place where the divine is to be found is not some or other heaven in another dimension, but in the realm of meta-information, the noosphere. The mind of this impersonal God encompasses all the eternal and universal axioms that rule and govern the universe and mankind.*

BIBLIOGRAPHY

Editions of the Holy Scriptures

Passages from the Bible are quoted from the *World English Bible* as found on a CD with the title *The Bible Collection, Deluxe Edition*, and published by ValuSoft, a division of THQ Inc, Waconia MN, 2002.

The above-mentioned CD also contains the Hebrew text of the Old Testament and the Greek text of the New Testament, as well as *Strong's Complete Greek & Hebrew Lexicon*. Other lexica utilised are mentioned under the heading of Other Literature.

In addition, the following editions of the biblical text in the original languages were consulted:

Elliger, K. and W. Rudolph, eds. *Biblia Hebraica Stuttgartensia.* Stuttgart: Deutsche Bibelgesellschaft, 1997.
Nestle, E. and E. Nestle, eds. *Novum Testamentum Graece.* Stuttgart: Deutsche Bibelstiftung, 1981.

The text of the Qur'an was consulted from the following translations:

Rodwell, J.M. and A. Jones, eds. *The Koran.* London: Phoenix, 1994.
Talal Itani, ed. *Quran in English, Modern English Translation.* https://blog.clearquran.com/download/

Other Literature

Allan, Alfred. *Law and Ethics in Psychology: An International Perspective*. Somerset West: Inter-Ed, 2008.

Allen, R.H. *Star Names: Their Lore and Meaning*. New York: Dover, 1963.

American Bill of Rights
http://www.archives.gov/exhibits/charters/bill_of_rights_transcript.html

American Psychiatric Association. *Diagnostic And Statistical Manual Of Mental Disorders, Fifth Edition: DSM-5*. Washington: American Psychiatric Publishing, 2013.

Aminoff, M.J. ed. *Encyclopaedia of the Neurological Sciences*. New York: Elsevier Science, 2003.

Anon. "First the Munchies then the Mania". *Medical Brief,* 18.02.2015. http://www.medicalbrief.co.za/archives/first-the-munchies-then-the-mania/

Aristotle: On The Heavens. Translated by J. L. Stocks. http://classics.mit.edu/Aristotle/heavens.html

Aquilecchia, G. "Bruno, Giordano". Chicago: Encyclopaedia Britannica, 2010.

Armstrong, Karen. *The Battle for God : Fundamentalism in Judaism, Christianity and Islam.* London: Harper Collins, 2001.

----. *The Bible: The Biography*. London: Atlantic, 2007.

----. *The Case for God: What Religion Really Means*. London: Vintage, 2010.

----. *Fields of Blood: Religion and the History of Violence*. London: Vintage, 2014.

----. *A History of God: From Abraham to the Present: The 4000-Year Quest for God*. London: Mandarin, 1994.

----. *Islam: A Short History.* London: Phoenix, 2009.

Arndt, W.F. and F.W. Gingrich. *A Greek-English Lexicon of the New Testament and Other Early Christian Literature*. Chicago: University of Chicago Press, 1957.

Augustine, Saint, Bishop of Hippo, *The Confessions.* Translated by E. B. Pusey (Edward Bouverie), 2002. https://www.gutenberg.org/files/3296/3296-h/3296-h.htm.

Barnes, J. "Plato". Chicago: Encyclopaedia Britannica, 2010.

Barrow, John. D. *The Artful Universe.* London: Penguin, 1995.

Belgic Confession, The https://www.crcna.org/welcome/beliefs/confessions/belgic-confession

Benedict, G. *The God Debate: A New Look at History's Oldest Argument.* London: Watkins, 2013.

Benzmüller, C and B.W. Paleo. "Experiments in Computational Metaphysics: Gödel's Proof of God's Existence". *Science and Spiritual Quest, 2015..* https://core.ac.uk/download/pdf/141495131.pdf.

Berggren, J.L. et al. "Mathematics". Chicago: Encyclopaedia Britannica, 2010.

Bird, O.A. "Kant, Immanuel". Chicago: Encyclopaedia Britannica, 2010.

Botha, M.E. *Metateoretiese Perspektiewe op die Sosiale Wetenskappe.* Potchefstroom: Departement Sentrale

Boudry, Martin. "The Sin of Scientism: Response to Clark". *Reports of The National Center for Science Education.* Sept–Oct 2015. Publikasie, PU vir CHO, 1993.

Burton, M. "Radiation.". Chicago: Encyclopædia Britannica, 2010.

Chadwick, B.A., H.N. Bahr, and S.L. Albrecht. *Social Science Research Methods.* Englewood Cliffs, N.J.: Prentic-Hall, 1984.

Churchwell, J.C. et al. "Altered Frontal Cortical Volume and Decision Making in Adolescent Cannabis Users". *Frontiers in Psychology,* 14 December 2010. http://journal.frontiersin.org/journal/10.3389/fpsyg.2010.00225/full.

Clark, P. et al. *Lippincott's Illustrated Reviews: Pharmacology.* Baltimore: Wolters Kluwer Health, 2012.

Clark, S. *The Big Questions: The Universe.* London: Quercus, 2010.

Collins, F. *The Language of God: A Scientist Presents Evidence for Belief.* London: Pocket, 2007.

Constitution of The Republic of South Africa, 1983. http://www.gov.za/documents/constitution/83cons.htm.

Constitution of The Republic of South Africa, 1996. https://www.justice.gov.za/legislation/constitution/saconstitution-web-eng.pdf

Cornelius, F. *Geistesgeschichte der Frühzeit II/1*. Leiden: Brill, 1962.

Cunningham, G.C. *Decoding the Language of God*. New York: Prometheus, 2010.

Davies, P. "Is There Need for a Divine Designer?" In *Secrets of Angels & Demons*, edited by D. Burstein and A. de Keijzer. London: Orion, 2005.

――――. "What Happened Before the Big Bang?" In *How Things Are: A Science Tool-Kit for the Mind*. Edited by J. Brockman and K. Matson. London: Phoenix, 2001.

Dawkins, Richard. *The God Delusion*. London: Bantam, 2006.

――――. *The Selfish Gene*. Oxford: Oxford University Press, 1976.

De Klerk, Willem. *Die Vreemde God en sy Mense*. Cape Town: Human & Rousseau, 1999.

Dennis, G. "Jewish Myth, Magic, and Mysticism". https://ejmmm2007.blogspot.com/2012/06/jews-and-zodiac-pt-1-good-sign.html.

Devenish, G.E. *A Commentary on the South African Bill of Rights*. Durban: Butterworths, 1999.

De Wet, J.J. et al. *Navorsingsmetodes in die Opvoedkunde: 'n Inleiding tot Empiriese Navorsing*. Durban: Butterworth, 1981.

Einstein, Albert. *Mein Weltbild*. Frankfurt a.M.: Ullstein, 1964.

――――. "Space-Time" (1926). (Reprinted in Encyclopaedia Britannica, 2010).

Ellenberg, Jordan. *Shape: The Hidden Geometry of Absolutely Everything*. London: Allen Lane, 2021.

Encyclopaedia Britannica. "Atom". Chicago: Encyclopædia Britannica, 2010.

――――. "Babylonian Exile". Chicago: Encyclopædia Britannica, 2010.

――――. "Consciousness". Chicago: Encyclopaedia Britannica, 2010.

――――. "Empedocles". Chicago: Encyclopædia Britannica, 2010.

――――. "Energy". Chicago: Encyclopædia Britannica, 2010.

-----. "Eratosthenes of Cyrene". Chicago: Encyclopædia Britannica, 2010.
-----. "Information Processing". Chicago: Encyclopædia Britannica, 2010.
-----. "Logos". Chicago: Encyclopædia Britannica, 2010.
-----. "Matter". Chicago: Encyclopædia Britannica, 2010.
-----. "Natural Law". Chicago: Encyclopaedia Britannica, 2010.
-----. "Tartarus". Chicago: Encyclopædia Britannica, 2010.
-----. "Teilhard de Chardin, Pierre". Chicago: Encyclopædia Britannica, 2010.
-----. "Uranus". Chicago: Encyclopædia Britannica, 2010.
-----. "Work". Chicago: Encyclopædia Britannica, 2010.
Esterhuyse, Willie. *God En Die Gode Van Egipte.* Wellington: Lux Verbi, 2009.
-----. *Sake-Etiek in die Praktyk*. Pretoria: J.L. Van Schaik, 1991.
Ferguson, Kitty. *The Fire in the Equations: Science, Religion & the Search for God*. Totonto: Bantam, 1995.
Flew, Antony. "Agnosticism". Chicago: Encyclopædia Britannica, 2010.
-----. *There Is A God: How the World's Most Notorious Atheist Changed his Mind*. New York: Harper Collins, 2007.
Frankl, Viktor Emil. *Das Menschenbild der Seelenheilkunde: Kritik des Dynaminschen Psychologismus*. Stuttgart: Hippocrates, 1959.
-----. 1959b. "Grundriβ der Existenzanalyse und Logoterapie". In *Handbuch der Neurosenlehre und Psychotherapie*, edited by V.E. Frankl, V.E. Von Gebsattel and J.H. Schultz. München: Urban & Schwarzenberg, 1959.
Friedlander, M.W. "Cosmic Ray". Chicago: Encyclopædia Britannica, 2010.
Galileo Galilei, *Dialogue Concerning the two Chief World Systems – Ptolemaic and Copernican,* 1630. Translated by Stillman Drake. Berkeley: University of California Press, 1967.
Garwood, Christine, *Flat Earth: The History of an Infamous Idea.* New York: Thomas Dunne, 2008.
Gauquelin, Michel. *Astrology and Science.* London: P. Davies, 1972.
Graffin, G. and S. Olson. *Anarchy Evolution: Faith, Science and Bad Religion*. New York: Harper Collins, 2010.

Grayling, A.C. *The God Argument: The Case Against Religion and for Humanism.* London: Bloomsbury, 2014.

Grundgesetz für die Bundesrepublik Deutschland. http://www.gesetze-im-internet.de/gg/bjnr000010949.html .

Hawking, Stephen and L. Mlodinow. *The Grand Design: New Answers to the Ultimate Questions of Life.* London : Bantam, 2011.

Heidelberg Catechism http://www.reformed.org/documents/heidelberg.html

Heim, Karl. 1957. *Christian Faith and Natural Science.* Translated by N.H. Smith. New York: Harper and Row, 1957.

————. *Glaube und Denken: Philosophische Grundlegung einer Christlichen Lebensanschauung.* Wuppertal: Aussaat, 1975.

Hengel, M. *Judentum und Hellenismus, Studien zu Ihrer Begegnung unter Besonderer Berücksichtigung Palästinas Bis zur Mitte des 2. Jh.s v. Chr.* Tübingen: Mohr Siebeck, 1973.

Heyns, Johan Adam. *Teologiese Etiek: Deel 1.* Pretoria: N.G. Kerkboekhandel Transvaal, 1982.

Heyns, Johan Adam and Willie D. Jonker. *Op Weg met die Teologie.* Pretoria: N.G. Kerkboekhandel, 1974.

Heyns, L.M. and H.J.C. Pieterse. *Eerste Treë in die Praktiese Teologie.* Pretoria: Gnosis, 1990.

Hillerbrand, H.J. "Luther, Martin". Chicago: Encyclopædia Britannica, 2010.

Hitchens, C. *God Is Not Great: The Case Against Religion.* London: Atlantic, 2007.

Horgan, J. *The End of Science: Facing the Limits of Knowledge in the Twighlight of the Scientific Age.* London: Abacus, 1998.

Humphreys, J. *In God We Doubt: Confessions of a Failed Atheist.* London: Hodder amd Stoughton, 2007.

Hyman, G. *A Short History of Atheism.* London: I.B. Tauris, 2010.

Jacobus, H.R. "The Zodiac Sign Names in the Dead Sea Scrolls (4q318): Features and Questions." *Aram,* 24 (2012) 311–31. file:///c:/users/user/downloads/the_zodiac_sign_names_in_the_dead_sea_sc.pdf.

Johnson, G. "Worshipping in Einstein's Church, or How I Found Fischbeck's Rule". In *Secrets of Angels and Demons*, edited by D. Burstein and A. de Keijzer. London: Orion. 2005.

Josephus, Flavius. *The Wars of The Jews, or History of the Destruction of Jerusalem*. Translated by W. Whiston. Project Gutenberg E-Book, 2009. https://www.gutenberg.org/files/2850/2850-h/2850-h.htm#link6noteref-20.

Joubert, Gideon. *Die Groot Gedagte: Abstrakte Weefsel van die Kosmos*. Kaapstad: Tafelberg, 1997.

Kenny, A.J.P. "Aristotle". Chicago : Encyclopaedia Britannica, 2010.

Kolb, B. and I.Q. Wishaw. *Fundamentals of Human Neuropsychology*. New York: Worth, 2009.

König, Adrio. "Daar is Soveel Sinlose Lyding op Aarde: Waar is God?" In *So Glo ons: Gelowig Nagedink oor God, die Bybel en ons Leefwêreld*, edited by P. Meiring et al. Vereeniging: Christelike Uitgewersmaatskappy, 2001.

─────. *Hier Is Ek!* Pretoria: N.G. Kerkboekhandel, 1975.

─────. "Teologie". In *Inleiding In Die Teologie*, edited by I.H. Eybers, A. König and J.A. Stoop. Pretoria: N.G. Kerkboekhandel, 1978.

Kuhn, T.S. *The Structure of Scientific Revolutions*. Chicago: The University of Chicago Press, 1970.

Küng, Hans. *Existiert Gott?* München: Piper, 1978.

─────. "Paradigm Change in Theology: A Proposal for Discussion". In *Paradigm Change in Theology: A Symposium for the Future*, edited by H. Kung and D. Tracy. New York: Crossroad, 1989.

Lambek, J. "Mathematics, Foundations of". Chicago: Encyclopaedia Britannica, 2010.

Lennick, D. and F. Kiel. *Moral Intelligence: Enhancing Business Performance and Leadership Success*. Upper Saddle River, NJ: Wharton School, 2008.

Malina, Bruce. *On the Genre and Message of Revelation: Star Visions and Sky Journeys*. Peabody Mass: Hendrickson, 1995.

McGregor, G.H.C. and A.C. Purdy. *Jew and Greek: Tutors unto Christ, the Jewish and Hellenistic Background of the New Testament*. London: Saint Andrew, 1959.

Mesarovic M.D. "Foundations for a General Systems Theory". In *Views On General Systems Theory, Proceedings of the Second Systems Symposium at Case Institute of Technology*. Edited by M.D. Mesarovic. New York: John Wiley, 1964.

Mills, D. *Atheist Universe: The Thinking Person's Answer to Christian Fundamentalism.* Berkeley, Ca: Ulysses, 2000.

Moser, M-B. and E.I. Moser. "Understanding The Cortex Through Grid Cells". In *The Future of the Brain: Essays by the World's Leading Neuroscientists* edited by G. Marcus and J. Freeman. Princeton : Princeton University Press, 2015.

Mouton, J. and H.C. Marais. *Basiese Begrippe: Metodologie van die Geesteswetenskappe.* Pretoria: RGN, 1992.

Nida-Rümelin, J. and W. Singer. "Erregungsmuster und Gute Gründe: Über Bewusstsein und Freien Willen". In *Zukunft Gehirn: Neue Erkenntnisse, Neue Herausforderungen*, edited by T. Bonnhoeffer and P Gruss. München, C.H. Beck, 2011.

Oakes, L. and L. Gahlin. *Ancient Egypt: An Illustrated Reference to the Myths, Religions, Pyramids and Temples of the Land of the Pharaohs.* London: Hermes, 2004.

Origenes Adamnatios. *Contra Celsum*. Translated by Phillip Schaff http://www.documentacatholicaomnia.eu/03d/0185-0254,_origenes,_contra_celsus,_en.pdf.

Paine, Thomas. *The Age of Reason*. London: Freethought Publishing Company, 1880. Facsimile published on the Internet at: http://www.gutenberg.org/files/3743/3743-h/3743-h.htm

Papineau, D. and H. Selina. *Introducing Consciousness.* Cambridge: Icon, 2006.

Perrin, N. "Bultmann, Rudof (Karl)". Chicago: Encyclopaedia Britannica, 2010.

Peters, F.E. *The Harvest of Hellenism, a History of the Near East from Alexander the Great to the Triumph of Christianity.* London: Barnes and Noble, 1972.

Pharmaceutical Manufacturers Association of SA and Another: In re Ex Parte President of the Republic of South Africa and Others 2000 (2) SA 674 (CC).

Philo of Alexandria. *On The Giants*. Translated by Charles Duke Yonge. http://www.earlychristianwritings.com/yonge/book9.html.
Pieterse, Hennie. *Praktiese Teologie as Kommunikatiewe Handelingsteorie*. Pretoria: RGN, 1993.
Pinker, Stephen. *The Blank Slate: The Modern Denial of Human Nature*. London: Penguin, 2003.
----. *How the Mind Works*. London: Penguin, 1997.
Plato. *Timaeus*. Translated by Benjamin Jowett http://classics.mit.edu/plato/timaeus.html
Polkinghorne, J. "The Nature of Time". In *On Space and Time,* edited by A. Majid. Cambridge: Cambridge University Press, 2008.
Ratey, J.J. *A User's Guide to the Brain: Perception, Attention, and the Four Theaters of the Brain*. London: Abacus, 2003.
Reader's Digest. *Southern African Word Power Dictionary: Improve your English as you Build your Vocabulary*. Cape Town: The Reader's Digest Association South Africa, 1996.
Rocke, A.J. "Chemistry". Chicago: Encyclopaedia Britannica, 2010.
Rousseau, Leon. *Die Groot Avontuur: Wondere van die Lewe op Aarde*. Kaapstad: Human & Rousseau, 2006.
Russel, P. *From Science to God: A Physicist's Journey into the Mystery of Consciousness*. Novato, Cal: New World Library, 2005.
Schagrin, M.L. "Logic". Chicago: Encyclopaedia Britannica, 2010.
Schilling, H.K. "The Threefold Nature of Science and Religion". In *Science and Religion: New Perspectives on the Dialogue*. Edited by I.G. Barbour. London: SCM, 1968.
Seiffert, H. *Einführung in die Wissenschaftstheorie: Erster Band*. München: C.H. Beck, 1972.
Shaw, P. *Logic and its Limits*. Oxford: Oxford University Press, Shermer, M. *The Believing Brain: From Ghosts and Gods and Conspiracies – How we Construct Beliefs and Reinforce them as Truths*. New York: St Martin's, 2011.
Sherry, P. "Theodicy". Chicago, Encyclopedia Britannica, 2010.
Siegel, E. "This is why the Multiverse Must Exist". *Forbes*, Mar 15, 2019. https://+/www.forbes.com/sites/startswithabang/2019/03/15/this-is-why-the-multiverse-must-exist/?sh=5c87cb196d08.
Singer, P. "Ethics". Chicago: Encyclopædia Britannica, 2010.

Smith, B.H. "Scientism". https://www.academia.edu/37984670/_scientism.

Springer, J.L. *Waar, Wat en Wie is God? De Vraag naar God als Godsdienst-Wijsgerig Probleem.* Wageningen: H. Veenman en Zonen, 1969.

Stenger, Viktor *The New Atheism: Taking a Stand for Science and Reason.* New York: Prometheus, 2009.

Stoker, H.G. *Beginsels en Metodes in die Wetenskap.* Johannesburg: Boekhandel De Jong, 1969.

Strauss, D.F.M. *Inleiding tot die Kosmologie.* Bloemfontein: Sacum, 1978.

Sztompka, P. *System and Function: Toward a Theory of Society.* New York: Academic, 1974.

Taylor, J.E. and D. Hay. "Astrology in Philo of Alexandria's De Vita Contemplativa: Paper Read at Aram Society for Syro-Mesopotamian Studies 29th International Conference on the Theme of Astrology in the Ancient Near East, Held at The University of Oxford, 08-10 July 2010". file:///c:/users/user/downloads/astrology_in_philo_of_alexandrias_de_vit.pdf

Thiel, R. *And then There was Light.* New York: Knopf, 1958.

Transman (Pty) Ltd v Dick and Another 2009 (4) SA 22 (SCA).

United Nations. "Universal Declaration of Human Rights, 1948". (Reprinted In Encyclopaedia Britannica, 2010).

Van Aarde, A.G. "A Commemoration of the Legacy of Rudolf Bultmann, Born 130 Years Ago". *Studia Historiae Ecclesiasticae*, Vol 40, No 1, 2014. https://uir.unisa.ac.za/handle/10500/13710

Van Helden, A. "Galileo". Chicago: Encyclopaedia Britannica, 2010.

Van Peursen, C.A. *De Opbouw van de Wetenschap: Een Inleiding in de Wetenschapsleer.* Amsterdam: Boom, 1980.

Visser, A.J. *De Openbaring aan Johannes.* Nijkerk: Callenbach, 1962.

Villanueva, J.C. "How Many Atoms are There in the Universe? http://www.universetoday.com/36302/atoms-in-the-universe/.

Von Mehren, A.T. "Contract". Chicago: Encyclopaedia Britannica, 2010.

Ward, Keith. *Is Religion Irrational?* Oxford: Lion Hudson, 2011.

Weinberg, Steven. *Dreams of a Final Theory: The Search for the Fundamental Laws of Nature.* London: Vintage, 1993.

Wells, R.B. "Mathematics and Mathematical Axioms". In *The Critical Philosophy and the Phenomenon of Mind.* Moscow, ID: University of Idaho, 2006.
https://webpages.uidaho.edu/rwells/Critical%20Philosophy%20and%20Mind/Contents%20and%20Preface.pdf

Westminster Confession of Faith
http://www.pcaac.org/wp-content/uploads/2012/11/wcfscriptureproofs.pdf.

Zee. A. Eintstein's Universe: Gravity at Work and Play. Oxford: Oxford University Press, 1989.

Zimmer, Carl. *Evolution.* London: Arrow, 2003.

Picture Credits

God as Architect of the Universe
 https://thomasguild.blogspot.com/2013/01/the-medieval-toolchest-compass-calliper.html.

The Beit Alpha Mosaic
 https://1.bp.blogspot.com/-0okrhto5gd0/t94a4giichi/aaaaaaaaaxs/z7wkosqedao/s1600/zodiac+2.jpg.

How Our Solar System Fits into the Bigger Picture of the Universe
 https://www.pinterest.com/pin/522558362987375677/visual-search/?x=0&y=0&w=362&h=894.

The Hebrew Conception of the Cosmos
 http://patrickschreiner.com/?cat=18

The Aristotelian Worldview
 http://www.chiron-center.com/worldview-studies

Frontispiece to Galileo's *Dialogo*
 Encyclopaedia Britannica, 2010, Galileo Galilei.

Plato
 https://www.britannica.com/biography/plato.

The Human Brain
 http://www.acbrown.com/neuro/lectures/assc/nrasscprfr.htm.

www.ingramcontent.com/pod-product-compliance
Lightning Source LLC
Chambersburg PA
CBHW060624250426
43670CB00056B/1958